Rigmaroles & Ragamuffins

*Unpicking words we
derive from textiles*

··· *Elinor Kapp* ···

Rigmaroles & Ragamuffins
Unpicking words we derive from textiles
© Elinor Kapp 2007
Published by Word4Word, Evesham, UK

ISBN 978-1-906316-00-6

The right of Elinor Kapp to be identified as the author of this work has been asserted by her in accordance with the Copyright, Designs and Patents Act 1988.

A copy of this publication has been registered with the British Library

Printed and bound by Cromwell Press, UK

Grateful acknowledgement is made to the following for permission to reprint previously published material.

Translation of an extract from the *Gudrunarkvida* on page 34 from *Cassell's Dictionary of Norse Myth and Legend* by Andrew Orchard. Reproduced courtesy of Cassell PLC, a division of The Orion Publishing Group (London).

Verses from *In the merry month of June* on page 143, courtesy of the Bridgend Library Information Service. This song is associated with Ned Clamper, a folksinger from the Gower peninsula near Swansea, but on this occasion was sung by Ben 'Blow' Whelan, and recorded by Patrick Tobin on March 3rd 1976 in the Ty Clyd Home for the Aged, Bargoed. A transcript can be found at http://www.ballinagree.freeservers.com/bbwhelan4.html

Translation of *Mi welais ferch o'r Ystrad* (I saw a girl from Ystrad) on page 145 by and courtesy of Barry Tobin.

··· *Rigmaroles & Ragamuffins* ···
Unpicking words we derive from textiles

··· *Foreword* ···

One of the fascinations of a living language is the way in which words quickly take on a life of their own and adapt themselves to situations far removed from their original utilitarian function. Our language is full of words and phrases that started life as part of the vocabulary of a particular trade or craft but are now transformed as part of our daily language. Freed from particular references, such phrases help to articulate and enrich the widest aspects of our human experience.

This is especially true of terms relating to textiles and their construction demonstrating the intimate and significant role that fabric and thread, weaving, spinning and embroidery play in our lives and our histories.

Drawing on her rich experience as a textile artist Elinor Kapp has delved into the meanings of words that she became familiar with as she came into contact with materials and processes often centuries old. In this wide ranging, informative and entertaining book Elinor makes an important contribution to our awareness of the cultural importance of textiles. Here is a linguistic journey through a fascinating world of materials, tools and processes shedding light on the forgotten origins of many words that are now part of our common language.

Alex Caprara
Co-Principal, Opus School of Textile Arts

··· *Rigmaroles & Ragamuffins* ···
Unpicking words we derive from textiles

··· *Dedication* ···

This book is dedicated to my dear family.

To my son Dr Rupert Rawnsley, my
daughter-in-law Erika Rawnsley and the children,
Alexander and Nathaniel, and to my daughter Amanda
Rawnsley and my son-out-law, Jon Foster.

Also to the memory of my late husband
Ken Rawnsley CBE.

• • •

Cover picture designed and embroidered by
Louise Gardiner

Illustrations by Adam Fisher

··· *Rigmaroles & Ragamuffins* ···
Unpicking words we derive from textiles

··· *Acknowledgements* ···

I would like to thank some of the many fellow enthusiasts who have helped me.

Julia and Alex Caprara, Kay Swancutt, Bea Sewell, Sheila Cahn and all at Opus School of Textile Arts, especially tutors Jane Elliott, Jacqueline Ansell and Margaret Hall Townley.

Jan Beaney and Jean Littlejohn. Claudine Joho.

Richard Berry, Cath Little, Guto Dafis, Amanda Rackstraw, Phil Anderson, Diana Morgan, David Ambrose, Nigel Davies, Steve Killick and Barry Tobin, from the Cardiff Storytelling Circle. Dr Robin Gwyndaf and Mrs Eleri Gwyndaf.

Storytellers Hugh Lupton, Eric Maddern, Gwdihw, Daniel Cohen, Robin, Bina and Vashti Williamson, and Steve Gladwin.

Friends Judy Roland, Richard Edge, Professor Paul and Mrs Gerri Ballard, Dilys Nilsson, Hannah Jones, Des Barry and Helen Williams, Alison Walker, Angie Luther, Ceri Shepherd, Ana Adnam, Professor Ronald Hutton, Hiroko Sue, Annabel Clemmo, Belinda Kembury, Sylvia Kapp, Alan and Renella Phillips, my brother John Kapp, The Reverend Dr Julie Hopkins, Joy Jones, Stephen Garrett, Dr Lata Mathur and Bryon Harrhy. Also the late and much-loved artist, Tony Goble.

My local stitching friends Kaye Edwards, Claire Grainger, Halina Davies, Mary Jenkins, Diana Palmer, Di Wise and Jaci Jones.

Alan and Margaret Leisk and Jan Woodward in Australia; Pat Gore in America; Michele de Santos in Brazil; Geeta Ramanujam in India; and Jasna Held in Bosnia.

··· *Rigmaroles & Ragamuffins* ···
Unpicking words we derive from textiles

··· *Contents* ···

··· *Rigmaroles & Ragamuffins* ···
Unpicking words we derive from textiles

··· *Rigmaroles & Ragamuffins* ···
Unpicking words we derive from textiles

Corduroy Road

Exchequer

Grasp the nettle

· · · *Introduction* · · ·

The English language has developed over many centuries from many diverse languages and cultures, some now lost. If we want to bring to life something of its impressive history, we might use the metaphor of a great river into which streams and rivulets constantly flow. Alternatively we could liken it to a mighty tree that has grown organically from buried roots, spreading out into a living canopy of innumerable and constantly renewed twigs and leaves.

My preference is to think of English as a wonderful piece of embroidery, stitched with a multitude of varied threads onto a base of primitive communication. The upper surface dazzles us with its range of colours, tones and textures. But to understand its construction, we need to take a look at the underside of the work. Here we can see the untidiness – the awkward seams, peculiar knots and frayed ends. In places, time has worn away our words to leave threadbare gaps; in others, swathes have been cut away by changing tastes and trends, allowing flamboyant new threads to be spliced in.

When we unpick the English language, it is quite startling to find how many of our common words, sayings, figures of speech, folklore, myths, nursery rhymes and stories come from thread and all the fascinating processes it had to go through to create textiles.

Rigmaroles and Ragamuffins is the result of my long involvement with textiles as an embroiderer and my recognition of the therapeutic potential in textile crafts. I am also fascinated by the way English weaves the threads of our past into today's figures of speech, bringing richly layered meaning to our lives.

· · · *Rigmaroles & Ragamuffins* · · ·
Unpicking words we derive from textiles

The textile-related words collected in this book are here because they have entered our everyday consciousness through spoken and written English. Many of the terms are still in use in their original practical sense to describe textile-related activities, as well as being used as metaphors and figures of speech. Others have somehow lost their craft connections entirely and acquired totally new meanings. Words are delightfully wayward things and sometimes go off in surprising directions.

Readers will notice that my collection includes the tools one needs to work with threads and cloth, such as needles and pins. We enthusiasts love everything to do with textiles. However, this book is most definitely not a general dictionary of terms. The words and phrases included here have had to earn their passage into the book by their usefulness or oddity as metaphors.

Rigmaroles and Ragamuffins is very simply constructed and easy to enjoy. The main entries appear in order of the first letter of the phrase or word. A hand (☞) indicates related terms that you might like to explore, so that you can browse through subjects that interest you. Thanks to its colourful patchwork of snippets of information and short stories, this is the ideal book to dip into between times when you are quilting, embroidering and so on.

When a word or phrase is being used in its everyday sense, describing textiles, it will be shown in ordinary lower case, like this sentence. ***Bold italics*** highlight words and phrases that are used figuratively or in common sayings, other than when these are used as part of a quotation. <u>Underlined type</u> is used to clarify the origin and meaning of words, or to make the tracing of complex derivations easier to follow.

Now, read on … and prepare to be amused and amazed.

··· *Rigmaroles & Ragamuffins* ···
Unpicking words we derive from textiles

Silkworm

Twister

Wind me round your finger

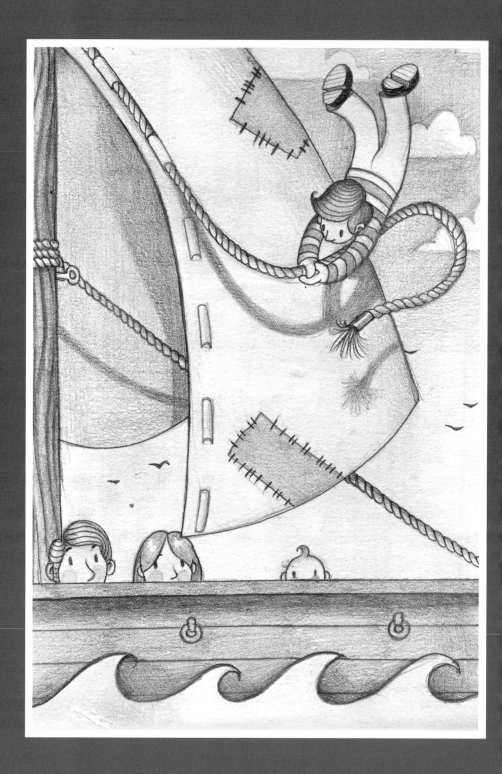

··· At a loose end ···

AT A LOOSE END ☞ ROPE, WHIP and YARN

If you see children mooching about, apparently doing nothing recognisably useful, you are likely to say they are *at a loose end*. Why not send the little dears off to sea on an old sailing ship? That is where the phrase was coined.

As with **spinning a yarn**, on quiet days at sea when the weather was good sailors would have to perform ordinary tasks. All the thousands of ropes or 'sheets' making up the rigging needed to have their ends bound with twine to prevent them fraying. Anyone with no other duties would be sent to **tie up the loose ends**.

I'm sure a spell of seasickness, repeated drenching in cold seawater and nothing but hard ship's biscuits full of weevils to eat would guarantee the children taking care to appear usefully employed at all times.

BAA BAA BLACK SHEEP ☞ FLEECE, SURNAME and WOOL

As most people know, the nursery rhyme **Baa Baa Black Sheep** is a political complaint about wool taxes in the Middle Ages. The hard working peasant had to give up a third of his wool to his feudal Master, a third to Mother Church, and only kept a third for himself.

> Baa Baa Black sheep, have you any wool?
> Yes sir, yes sir, three bags full.
> One for the Master, and one for the Dame,
> And one for the little boy who lives down the lane.

There have been repeated suggestions in the popular press that over-sensitive local councils in England have attempted to ban this nursery rhyme, on the grounds that the stereotyping of black sheep with a negative image was insulting to black people. Whenever this is repeated, there is a storm in the media, which usually results in a report that the edict has been reversed. The whole story is, however, a good example of an urban myth. It was first reported in the press in the mid-1980s, and its progress over the next two decades has been well charted. We seem to need daft examples of so-called political correctness in order to make us feel superior in our tolerance and sophistication. I must admit that I myself was totally taken in and believed this story for years, tut-tutting over 'loony-left councils' along with the rest of the gullible public.

I am sure, therefore, that we are still allowed to call someone **the black sheep of the family**, referring to a relative who has lived a bad or wicked life. This phrase has been used in colloquial speech for a rascal since the late 18th century.

There are lots of contradictory superstitions regarding black sheep. In some places the birth of a black lamb was regarded as lucky for the family, in others it was a portent of ill fortune, even death, and had to be killed at once.

The origin of the word sheep is lost, but seems to be West Germanic, and to have spread in slightly different forms – sceap, schaf, schaap – through most European languages. It is possible that it derives from German schaffen, meaning to make or create, which would link it to the English word **shape**.

While we debate this, the hardworking sheep, white or black, who has already given up her woolly coat, is lucky if she escapes being **fleeced** to provide leather for clothes, packs, bags, thongs, tents, parchment to write on, and milk, cheese and meat for food; not to mention tallow for candles. It's probably lucky that sheep are not as politically active as peasants.

Good animal husbandry pays off in the long run. As an Albanian proverb says (or maybe doesn't, since many spoof Albanian proverbs have been invented by the humorist Miles Kington), 'a skinned sheep gives no milk'. Whether coined by gnarled Eastern European peasant or modern joker, it's a good proverb, and the Romans in the 1st century BC would certainly have agreed. They are said to have sometimes dressed their sheep in coats to keep the fleece really soft and the sheep really happy.

We know from the Bible that **the lost sheep** represents most of us sinners who are liable to stray from the path of virtue. It is a metaphor for sin and salvation in the Christian tradition, but fortunately the **good shepherd** is tirelessly seeking us.

We have looked at sheep as helpless little victims, all timid and **sheepish**, a word used to describe someone who is awkward, simple or silly, or abashed at being in unfamiliar company. On the other hand, **a wolf in sheep's clothing** is the opposite, and describes someone concealing aggressive or wicked intentions by lulling the victim into a false sense of security. We know this phrase from one of Aesop's fables (which tells of a wolf who covered himself with a sheep's fleece in order to sneak up on the flock unobserved), yet a similar figure of speech must have been known long before Aesop. Jesus, who drew His parables from common experience, warned, 'Beware of false prophets, which come to you in **sheep's clothing**, but inwardly they are ravening wolves.'

BALL OF THREAD ☞ CLUE and THREAD

The idea of the sun as *a ball which is spun every morning out of light* was very much part of Celtic spirituality. 'Soul teacher, weaver of my soul, send forth your shining ball of thread, that I may follow the track of this day's turning,' says one early Celtic prayer. Such a concept may well go back to the days of ancient Greece, when goddesses were renowned for their spinning. Circe, known best from Homer's *Odyssey*, was the daughter of Helios the sun god, and used to spin sunbeams for him every morning – at least, when she could spare the time from seducing Odysseus and turning his men into swine ('Just hang on for a moment, dad, while I bring home the bacon').

BAND ☞ BIND, BOND, SHAFT, TIE and TWINE

In medieval Latin, banda was a scarf and bandum a banner, or scarf-like flag. A band can go round your waist as a belt, or round your hat, and means any narrow strip of fabric. A *bandage* is a narrow strip for binding up wounds, and **to band** something is to mark it in stripes, as if by a thread wound round it.

People who are **bound** together in a common purpose are called **a band**. If you decide to be **a band of robbers** it would be better if you didn't try to be **a brass band** at the same time; it might be tricky maintaining the silence and stealth required for robbing people.

BASTE ☞ SEW

There was a word in Old French, bastir, meaning to sew something with bast, a word derived from a lost Germanic root. Bast was probably originally fibres of bark but by the middle of the 15th century referred to string or rope. The Americans still refer to basting, meaning making a series of loose, temporary stitches, which we English call tacking.

Although the basting done to a roast joint of meat has no connection with textiles, the other uses of the word all do, because the bastiz, meaning plant fibre, was thrashed and heckled to make thread. A *bastinado* was a rod used in medieval Spain for torturing prisoners and criminals by beating them on the soles of the feet. In the 16th century, the same word, **baste** or **baist**, meant to thrash someone, and became generally accepted, though not considered very polite.

The word **lambast** derives from combining bast with an old Scandinavian root, lam, also meaning to thrash or cripple someone – a kind of double beating. In other situations, to lam could mean to break by hitting, linked with lame. It was also a dialect word for a <u>blade</u>, connecting it to weaving, and the same word, <u>lam</u>, is used for the blade-like pieces of wood connecting the loom to its treadles. Tailors used a lot of slang terms, almost like another language. One term was to <u>baist a snarl</u> meaning to <u>work up a quarrel</u>.

As we sit gently sewing, we should reflect on these aggressive connections and perhaps consider that we are getting some really vigorous exercise without having to leave the comfortable sofa at all.

BEAD ☞ BUTTON

Another way of embellishing stitched fabric is to incorporate beads. Ornaments stitched onto clothing are among the oldest forms of decoration, being found in many prehistoric burials. The earliest known examples are pierced shells, dated to 100,000 years ago.

We don't really know what they might have been called in prehistoric times, since our word <u>bead</u> really means a <u>prayer</u>. Does this suggest that personal adornment and religious meaning were not separated until historic times? Beads were also used for the abacus, beads strung on a frame and used for calculations by the Chinese, as long ago as 3,000 BC.

The earliest word we have for a <u>bead</u> is the Germanic <u>beth</u>, which entered Old English as <u>gebed</u>, a <u>prayer</u>. Using a string of beads to count or regulate a series of prayers led to the association of the word for prayer with the small pierced marker; then, in the 13th century, the prefix <u>ge</u> dropped off and rolled into a dusty corner, never to be used again. A holy man paid to say prayers for other people was a <u>bedesman</u>, but more than a century passed before <u>bead</u> was used regularly in the modern sense to describe any small <u>decorative shape pierced with a hole</u>.

Anything similar to a bead can be used figuratively. We speak of **beads of sweat**, and something with an edge of repeated globular mouldings is **a beaded edge**. Someone with a bright eye and piercing glance might be described as having **a beady eye**, as in the jocular **I'm keeping my beady eye on you**!

Bead lightning is a rare and mysterious phenomenon that has the appearance of a string of beads in the sky for a few seconds following a bolt of lightning. It was once known as **St Martin's beads**.

A proverb from Persia says **the best rosary is the thread of life hung with the beads of love**. Amen to that.

Oh, what a bind! we might say of some tiresome task. Anything that acts as a tie or restraint on one's freedom, such as an obligation or a law, can mean you are *bound* to obey. We speak of *a binding promise* or say we are *bound by convention* or *precedent*. It applies to anything you must do, whether you want to or not, or a tie that should not or cannot be broken. *Bound over to keep the peace* is a legal term enshrining this idea.

Binding comes from a very early Indo-European root, conjectured to be bhendh because of the Sanskrit bandh, for bind, and the related Greek word peisma for cable. As a verb meaning to make fast with a tie or a knot, and to bond or fasten, it has also given a name to various climbing plants, such as *bindweed* and *woodbine* which appear to knot themselves round trees. *Bine* and *twine* are both nouns meaning string, and a *bundle* is something bound. The past participle was bunden, from which comes the old-fashioned term *your bounden duty*.

With some sense of inevitability we might say *it's bound to rain on the day of the garden party* or any other outdoor event that demands a dry day. *Bound up with* suggests being linked in a close association.

The proverb *fast bind, fast find* tells us that being careful and orderly makes life easier because you won't lose things – oh, I do so wish I could take that one to heart!

Books are *bound* too, as if the poor things were tied up, struggling, on the shelves, and *bookbinding* is both a process and an occupation. Originally, books were sewn into their bindings. While some are still stitched, others have pages held in place with glued canvas. We use the same words to explain the uniting of all those separate pages even when no thread is involved, as when producing paperbacks.

We can thank William Caxton, the first man to popularise printing, for another thread connection with books, since he started out in life as a cloth merchant.

There are ancient words that have ended up in English as bound, but do not have the connection to binding with thread. Bounds originally came from bodina, meaning a landmark in medieval Latin, and can be used in the sense of limits to an area of land. Beating the bounds is a ceremony of marking these out, and a boundary is the line showing the limit.

BOBBIN ☞ WEAVE

Once weaving became mechanised, the loom had rows of bobbins on which different colours were wound, going up and down in sequence at the same time as the automatic shuttle raced across. A children's rhyme with actions introduces children to the old techniques.

> Wind the bobbin up, wind the bobbin up,
> Pull, pull, pull, {clap, clap, clap}
> Wind it back again, wind it back again,
> Pull, pull, pull, {clap, clap, clap}

It would be a shame to lose these traditional rhymes, even though they might be more relevantly replaced by verses about moving a mouse around to bring up images and words on a computer monitor.

To bob was to go up and down, of unknown origin, but it seems likely that it gave the name to the weaver's bobbin, through the French bobine, in the 15th century. **Bobbing and weaving** is a term derived from this, used in the sport of boxing to mean moving up and down and from side to side, and suggesting that you are on your toes, trying to keep out of trouble by being alert and taking evasive action against life's blows. **Bobbing up and down** is used both literally and as a figure of speech for people getting up and down frequently from their seats.

For some reason **you're talking bobbins** is a way of saying you are talking nonsense. Perhaps the **thread** of your discourse is just going round and round and getting all tangled up.

BODKIN ☞ BUTTON

Hamlet, pondering the meaninglessness of life, speaks of 'A man being able his quietus to make with a bare bodkin.' Hamlet meant that he could commit suicide and find peace by stabbing himself, as a bodkin meant originally a small dagger, and is probably a diminutive of the Welsh word for such a weapon, a bidog.

A bodkin was once an essential tool for everyone. This sharply pointed implement with a fairly thick shaft was used to make round holes in shoes or clothes wherever a closure was necessary. Until buttons were invented, strings were threaded through these holes and tied.

While bodkins are still used by stitchers, particularly to pierce leather and other tough fabrics, they are almost obsolete otherwise – and probably classed as an offensive weapon nowadays. I think that's a pity really, as carrying one in your work bag conveys a very dashing image.

Sitting bodkin was used in the past to describe someone squashed between two others on a seat a little too narrow, as in a coach.

The old-fashioned oath <u>Ods Bodkins</u> was a corruption of 'God's bodykins' or 'God's dear body,' and has nothing to do with sewing.

BOMBASTIC

Someone with an inflated idea of his own importance might talk in a puffed-up way, using little-known words of many syllables to try to sound wise and important, but without much substance to his conversation. We would then describe him as *bombastic*, to show how much cleverer we can be.

The root word, <u>bombace</u>, was simply a word for <u>silk</u>, taken directly from the Greek <u>bombux</u>, which gave us the scientific name of the silkworm, *Bombyx mori*. By the 17th century, <u>bombast</u> was no longer silk: the term was applied to <u>cotton wool</u>, which is what <u>raw cotton</u> straight from the plant was called in Britain, imported from India and resembling <u>sheep's wool</u>. It was used for padding and stuffing doublets and other garments, particularly to enlarge the shoulders, crotch, or whatever bit of anatomy was fashionable at the time. The metaphorical use of *bombast* derived from this process of inflating a garment to enhance its owner's assets.

BOND ☞ BAND, BIND, SHAFT, TIE and TWINE

These are all words linked with thread as <u>something that unites and ties</u>, and came to us via Middle English as a variation on <u>band</u>.

Bonds are legal documents, such as promissory notes and securities. We say *his word is his bond* when we refer to an honourable man who does what he promises. *Bonded* means something held or secured, and a *bondholder* is the person who holds it, such as a tenant. The obligations and limitations of marriage are often spoken of figuratively as *the bonds of matrimony* and *family bonds*. *Bonded* can be used figuratively for anything that unites or binds in an abstract way, and all the emotions, both good and bad, that hold us together.

In earlier times, the condition of a slave or a serf in the Middle Ages was that of being bound legally as a possession, described as *bondage*. Nowadays, when outright slavery has mostly vanished, the word *bondage* tends to suggest sex, perhaps someone tied up in leather or other constraints during sadomasochistic practices.

There is a fashion nowadays for groups of people, from professions or companies, to get together for **corporate bonding** in trendy workshops, where they can have a day off work, act out their fantasies and covertly insult their superiors under the guise of therapy. Now that I think about it, there's quite a bit of sadomasochism in all that, but not quite so much leather.

BORN TO THE PURPLE

If you had been born in Roman times you would have wished you had been **born to the purple**. The Romans reserved purple cloth for the aristocracy, and the phrase refers to edicts in ancient Rome decreeing that the male heir to the reigning Emperor should be born in a room specially prepared with purple drapes. The newborn boy would be wrapped in purple cloth to show how special he was. I wonder what happened if the baby turned out to be a girl? Best not to enquire perhaps. Even today, the Queen of England wears purple robes and the term **the Royal purple** suggests something exclusive.

Would you believe it, a dog discovered the earliest purple dye. In the ancient world, purple dye could only be gained from crushed molluscs, *Murex trunculus*, from the Mediterranean, and hundreds were needed for even a small quantity of dye. The mythical hero Hercules, the strongest man in the world, unfortunately suffered a fit of madness in which he killed his friend Iphitus, and was sentenced by the gods to serve Queen Omphale for three years. While in her service, he had to wear a woman's dress and spin wool with her handmaidens, while Omphale wore his lion skin (what a come-down for a superhero). Hercules had a faithful sheepdog, and one day it came to him pouring reddish purple saliva from its jaws. It had bitten a seashell and revealed the murex dye. I can understand Hercules' momentary alarm. My little lap dog, Peri, once ate all the red papier mâché baubles off the Christmas tree, and came to me slavering with what appeared to be blood. She also survived.

The way to make a reliable chemical version of purple dye was only discovered – equally by accident – in the 19th century, as a by-product of coal tar. The discovery of aniline dyes by Sir William Perkin underwhelmed fellow chemists. But when Queen Victoria wore the new colour, mauve, to her daughter's wedding, it became an instant fashion item.

The moon shines bright,
The stars give light,
And little Nanny Button-cap
Will come tomorrow night.

Just a simple child's rhyme recited by Yorkshire children but it contains a folk-memory of Nanna the Norse moon goddess, wife of Baldur. What her connection could be to buttons is a bit of a mystery, but a full moon looks like a big silver or pearl button.

Buttons didn't link up with clothing till quite late on, the name coming from the Vulgar Latin botone, and then the Old French bouton, with the meaning of thrusting outwards. The same word gave us buds on a stem, still found in the term button mushroom, and the word butt, meaning to hit with the head. The idea of something thrusting upward only gradually developed into its use as a fastening, because in earlier times clothes were tied with strings or pinned together.

Although buttons have been around since prehistoric times, as museum artefacts show, they did not really take off as fastenings in the West until the 11th century. In fact it was the late invention of the buttonhole that held things back. At first, stud-like buttons, pushed through a hole or loop, were only used by men, and were usually very elaborate and ornamental; only in the 19th century did they become fully fashionable for women. India developed fastenings with buttons a lot earlier. Shirts were double-pierced and fastened with buttons resembling cufflinks, with a shaft and stud.

A **button-hole** is a flower or small nosegay that can be put through the buttonhole of a man's jacket, but also can be pinned onto the lapel.

There are minor different versions of the saying **to buttonhole someone**, and it may have been originally **to buttonhold him**. In the 18th century you might slip a finger into a man's buttonhole to detain him discreetly or, alternatively, hold onto him by the shank buttons standing proud from his coat. The term changed to develop the meaning of talking to someone who doesn't really want to listen, either because you're a bore, or are trying to tell him something he'd really rather not hear.

Button your lip is an obvious command to keep silent, and we refer to a reserved or secretive person as **buttoned up**.

A proverb about being careful of the company you keep is **gold buttons cannot belong on a torn coat**. Many buttons were made of metal – not necessarily gold, but bright when new and polished, and so we might say of someone that they are **as bright as a button**, meaning intelligent, smart, clever.

Hardly surprisingly, there are many sexually explicit slang expressions to do with buttons and buttonholes, because of their obvious analogy to human anatomy.

A **button nose** is descriptive of a small snub type of nasal protuberance, while **buttons** was a generic name for a page boy. He was a flunkey or youngster who performed lots of menial tasks in a hotel, the name referring to the rows of showy fastenings on his uniform. The character **Buttons**, Cinderella's confidant in the traditional pantomime, is the best-known use of the name.

I don't care a brass button arrived in the early 15th century, but **you've lost a button**, or **you're a button short** meaning craziness or foolishness is more recent.

CABBAGE ☞ ODDS AND ENDS

A real textile oddity is the use of the term **cabbage** to mean small pieces of cloth stolen by tailors, or small profits taken in kind as cloth. It originated in the 17th century, maybe from garbage, now meaning general rubbish, but originally animal and fish entrails. Apparently garbage is unrelated both to the verb to garb, meaning to clothe, and to garb, a noun embracing your style or the way you are clothed. Garb in that sense came from an Old High German root meaning adornment, and became grace or elegance in the mid 17th century. The term **cabbage** to describe small leftover pieces of fabric is still in use in the textile trade.

CAT'S CRADLE ☞ CORD, STRING and THREAD

That's got into a right cat's cradle you might say, looking at the mess in my workbasket or drawer, as if a kitten had been at play with a ball of wool. You might even say it, derisively, of my confused thoughts.

There are many string games that can be played by forming loops and shapes and then passing the taut strings between the hands of two or more individuals. These games can be found all over world and among all peoples, from the Australian Aborigines to the Navaho Indians in South-western America. In Western cultures, we call these string patterns a **cat's cradle**. No one really knows why, but one of the more plausible explanations links the word to the cradle or supporting framework of timbers on which a ship is constructed. A <u>cat</u> or <u>catt</u> was a type of merchant ship used in the 17th century, which might explain why the term <u>cat's cradle</u> made it to the transatlantic trading centres of New England very early. The term soon came to mean a <u>muddle of threads</u> or a <u>jumble of ideas</u>.

The Inuit play a very elaborate version, using a long loop of sealskin thong wound round the thumb and little fingers. They can make a seemingly endless number of designs, which are given traditional, if fanciful, descriptive names. They accompany each pattern by a song or poem. In this way, they preserve the legends and folklore of their hunting and fishing culture through a kind of tangible metaphor using thread pictograms with designs such as caribou running up a hill, birds, animals, people, sledges and boats. There are taboos against playing at certain seasons of the sun; break this rule and bad weather will follow. Sometimes thong games are forbidden to young boys for fear that, when they grow up, their fingers might tangle in a harpoon line, dragging them under the ice to their deaths. As with so many things that have become mere children's games to us, such textile rituals retain their magic potency in many other cultures.

CHIFFONNIER ☞ RAG

What do you think a small piece of deep-fried potato has in common with a chest of drawers? Chewing your way through a large wooden cabinet smothered in vinegar is probably not what you intended when you set out to buy some *fish and chips*.

However, a <u>chip</u> probably started off as <u>a piece cut off</u>, such as the branch of a tree. In Old English, <u>cippan</u> had a very specialised meaning, <u>the beam of a plough</u>. In the 15th century, <u>chip</u> had shifted to signifying <u>the crust off a loaf</u>, and by the 18th century, it meant to <u>break off</u>, rather than to <u>cut</u>. Fried <u>potato chips</u>, which perversely were cut, not broken, became the rage in Britain from the 1860s onward.

So, where's the textile link? Well, in Old French the word was <u>cipe</u>, which then became <u>chiffe</u>, a <u>rag</u>, and in French a <u>chiffonnier</u> is a <u>rag picker</u>. The English not only took over the word, in its later French embodiment of <u>chiffon</u>, a light, gauzy fabric, but also adopted the *chiffonnier* in the early 19th century. By this, they gained a <u>chest of drawers used to store odds and ends</u> – perhaps even a rag or two.

CHINTZY

This is a word we imported from India in the early 17th century, along with the painted calico that it described. The Hindi word was chint, but that wasn't quite classy enough for the East India merchants, so they elaborated it to chintz. The calico fabric was painted with small spot designs of flowers and birds, and chint meant just that – a spot or mark, derived from the spotted animal, the cheetah. The word also became chit or chitty, for a certificate or pass in Anglo-Indian, perhaps from the spot made by the official stamp.

Chintz is still decorated with flowers and birds of traditional Indian design, but the cotton ground is printed in a variety of colours, and it has a glazed surface suitable for furnishing fabric. In Britain today, **Chintzy** would suggest something pretty and expensive but a little old-fashioned. In the USA, **Chintzy** means more of a cheap compromise, as in **their quality is really chintzy**.

CLOBBER

In the 19th century, clobber meant clothes, but originally it came from the Yiddish klbr. To cobber up, without the l, was tailor's slang for to patch up.

Today **clobber** is used for any old junk. If I were to say – as I undoubtedly should – that I must clear all the clobber out of my house, I have to tell you that it would NOT include a cull of my wardrobe. Geddoffit! Leave-my-clothes-alone!

CLOTH ☞ FABRIC, MADE UP OUT OF WHOLE CLOTH, MATERIAL and STUFF

The word cloth is a little mysterious. In the forms of the plural clothes and the verb to clothe it was unknown before the 12th century. Its only known link with English comes via kleid, the German for garment, though in Old English a clout was a patch to put on a worn garment. It seems strange that the first of the three Fates, the spinner, is called Clotho or Klotho, yet none of the authorities I consulted suggested any connection to the textile word.

You can be metaphorically **clothed** in all sorts of things: shame, righteousness, glory, beauty and many more. The landscape can be **clothed** with snow or mist.

Sometimes we refer to people in a sort of shorthand, using their attire to describe them. **The cloth** now refers only to the clergy, in a rather pompous way, but in the early 19th century, when it was coined, it meant any member of a profession who wore a distinctive type of clothing.

Old King Cole was a merry old soul,
And a merry old soul was he.
He called for his pipe and he called for his bowl,
And he called for his fiddlers three.

What has that nursery rhyme got to do with textiles, you ask? Well, in the 16th century, there was very wealthy clothier – a merchant who makes and sells cloth – called Richard Colebrook of Reading. The rhyme may refer to him, as he was well known, and could have been nicknamed 'King' Cole, rather as we talk of 'Captains of Industry'.

CLOUT ☞ PATCH and RAG

In Old English, a clout was a patch, put over a hole to mend it. Later, in the Middle Ages, the word became applied to a rag, or any piece of fabric that could be slapped on in a hurry. The word had a link with blows, but also with clot, clod and lump. The dialect term, clouted cream, refers to cream thickened by scalding. As **clotted cream** it is a typical Cornish delicacy.

There is a country saying which goes

Cast not a clout
Till May be out.

You are being advised to keep your warm clothes on until late in the year, though no one is sure whether May means the month or the May-bush that flowers in spring. Alternatively, if you had a friend named May, you might not be able to undress for bed till she left the house. That's the trouble with country wisdom; it can mean anything.

You might fetch me a **clout** round the head for my silliness (please don't) but the use of the word to mean a blow only came in during the 14th century, and it's possible it has different parentage.

23

CLUE ☞ BALL OF THREAD

Who would have thought that a **ball of thread** would give us that staple of detective fiction, the **clue**? Yet every time we use this word we are recalling the famous story from Classical Greece, when a ball of thread was given by Ariadne to Theseus to help him find his way through the labyrinth. The hero Theseus was sent from mainland Greece to Crete to be sacrificed to the Minotaur, a terrible monster placed by King Minos in the heart of a maze. However, Ariadne, the King's daughter, fell in love with Thesus. She gave him a sword and a ball of thread to unroll on his way in, so that, having killed the Minotaur, he could find his way out again.

The word **clue** was originally spelt **clew**. Its origins relate to curling up in a ball, but it came to mean especially both a ball of thread and the action of tracking with a thread to find the way, and hence a hint or special fact that helps to find out the truth.

Writers of detective fiction certainly use the term, but we also say colloquially I **haven't a clue** to show we are totally at a loss, or we rudely say to someone acting stupidly that **you're absolutely clueless**.

The older spelling still survives. A **clew** is a little hole with a metal eyelet in the mainsail of a sailing ship, through which the control sheet is threaded, so that the sail can be tightened or loosened according to the wind. It can refer to the corner of the sail in which the eyelet is found, thus drawing up the sail is **to clew up**.

CORD ☞ CORDON, ROPE, SMALL STUFF, STRING, THREAD, TOW and YARN

As befitting something so useful, there are many synonyms for thread. Any structure twisted together can be referred to as either cord or string – they are almost the same, but cord is usually thought of as thicker and stronger than string. The Latin chorda for string became the word cord in Middle English for several strands of fibre twisted together. Indeed, any structure formed like this is named as a cord, such as the anatomical structures of the spermatic and umbilical cords.

Prehistoric people used cords made from cut strips of hide or dried animal intestines, which can be surprisingly strong and durable; they are still used in this way in some parts of the world. Early musicians must have discovered the musical twang from cords that were stretched and plucked, and some modern stringed instruments are still strung with various forms of gut. We also speak of and with our **vocal cords**.

Although the string of a musical instrument has been known as a <u>cord</u> since the 15th century, rather confusingly the melodic <u>chord</u>, where several harmonising notes are played together, probably came from a different source <u>accord</u>. This is connected to the Latin <u>cor</u>, for <u>heart</u>. Although they come from different roots, the semantic link may have helped establish the word <u>chord</u>. We say a sympathetic message **strikes a chord** with us, which could refer either to the <u>musical string</u> or the <u>sense of heartfelt accord</u>.

A **cord** is a measure of stacked wood, 8 feet by 4 feet by 4 feet (in metric, an inelegant 2.44 m by 1.22 m by 1.22 m), the name derived from the cord-like appearance of the stack. A smokeless explosive developed in the 18th century was named **cordite**, because it too came in bundles.

The word **cordage** is the formal collective term for the thinner ropes in a ship's rigging, and has been used since at least the late 15th century in a metaphorical way for the **threads of life**, though it has gone out of use now.

But when we say of someone overly dependent or neurotically fixated on their mother that they **can't cut the cord**, we refer to the umbilical one, the first and most vital form of connection in the life of every one of us, since without its work I would not be here to write, nor you to read these words.

··· *Corduroy Road* ···

CORDON ☞ CORD

Not surprisingly, a **cordon** came from <u>cord</u>, as a **cordon** in Old French was <u>stonework</u>, built up line by line, as a <u>defensive fortification</u>. It then began to mean a <u>line of soldiers</u> positioned in a row, on guard. From that it was not so far to become an <u>area for defence</u> – even one empty of anything, such as you would devise to prevent the spread of infection, or as a firebreak. In such circumstances, you might find an area of the town **cordonned off** to prevent anyone going there.

The military use of the word **cordon** came to us from France and, in the 19th century, we also got <u>cordonnet</u> from them meaning a <u>smaller version of cord</u>. This term fell out of use in the UK, but is now applied to a <u>thick cord of loosely spun silk</u> used in white work embroidery.

Also from France we get **cordelier**, a nickname for a strict order of Franciscan monks, referring to the knotted cord they wear to symbolise their vows.

CORDUROY ☞ CORD

If you thought a ride on a **corduroy road** would be nice and gentle, you'd be in for a shock. The textile known as corduroy has a pile raised in a series of cord-like ribs along its surface, and is usually a tough cotton or woollen stuff for workers' clothes. It came in during the 18th century and may have originally been made in ribbed silk. The name seems to have come from <u>cord</u> plus <u>duroy</u> or <u>deroy</u> and, according to one authority, is derived from the French <u>Cord du Roi</u>, meaning <u>King's Cord</u>, though this isn't entirely convincing.

Laying logs down in parallel rows on swampy ground was found to be a good way of building roads in pioneering countries, and these rough tracks resembled the ribbed cloth. In the 19th century, they were therefore called **corduroy roads**, and would surely have given you an undignified and bumpy ride.

COTTON

The playwright Congreve has one of his characters say, 'I love to see 'em hug and cotten together, like Down upon a Thistle.' Fluffy threads like those of <u>cotton</u> and <u>thistledown</u> hold together, and cling to other surfaces.

The word <u>cotton</u>, from the Arabic <u>qutn</u>, came to Europe by way of the Spanish Moors in the 14th century, and into English from Old French <u>coton</u>. **Cottoning on to** something meant <u>harmonising</u> and <u>prospering</u> in the 16th century, when it was derived from the successful <u>raising of the nap</u> or pile <u>on cotton cloth</u>.

Nowadays we say **cotton on to** an idea, as it has come to mean to <u>embrace</u> or <u>be drawn</u> to something, and we **cotton on to a person** when we <u>take a liking to them</u>.

Cotton is the fluffy seed head of a plant grown in hot climates such as those of India, Africa and the Southern states of the USA, and it has always been a very valuable source of thread. It was probably cultivated in India over 5,000 years ago, and in Classical Greece a little later. By the 1st century AD Arab traders had brought cotton to Europe, although it was not in common use in the UK until trade with India took off in the 17th century. Pliny the Elder, the Roman scholar, mentions it in his *Historia Naturalis*, written before 77 AD.

> *There grows a shrub which some call gossypium. It is small and bears a fruit resembling the filbert, within which is downy wool which is spun into threads, there is nothing to be preferred to these stuffs for softness and whiteness. Beautiful garments are made from them for the priests of Egypt.*

Cotton-tail is a name for the common rabbit, presumably because their cute little tails look like the fluffy cotton as it grows on the plant. It has gained currency in naturist circles to describe someone whose buttocks are whiter than their back and legs, with a presumed resemblance to the rabbit's tailpiece and showing that they have been sunbathing wearing a costume.

The cartoon character Bugs Bunny uses the catchphrase **just a cotton-pickin' minute!** meaning 'hold on a moment' while he makes another wildly impossible escape. **In high cotton** means in good times, easy pickings, as the cotton bolls were high and plentiful on the stalks in the plantations of America. However, this can be a sensitive term because of the links with slavery, and calling someone a **cotton picker** would be highly offensive today.

Raw cotton was an ideal cheap soft packing material, so to **keep someone in cotton wool** is to overprotect them. Nowadays we use polystyrene chips or bubblewrap for this purpose, but so slow are figures of speech to change that we don't hear about 'keeping someone in polystyrene chips'. We would have a momentary shock if we did, though it would make just as much sense.

Cotton was responsible for one of the World's Biggest Mistakes. When Columbus set sail from Spain across the Atlantic, he was hoping to find a better trade route to the Orient, and cotton was definitely one of the goods he wanted to acquire. What he couldn't know, of course, was that, far from waiting to be discovered, America was well populated and, what's more, cotton was thriving in Santo Domingo (now the Dominican Republic) in the Caribbean when he arrived. Seeing the people there dressed in clothes of cotton, Columbus was immediately convinced that he had succeeded in reaching the Far East or the Indies. We still celebrate his mistaken assumption by referring to the islands of this region as the West Indies.

CROSSPATCH ☞ PATCH, PIECING and QUILT

> *Cross patch, draw the latch,*
> *Sit by the fire and spin;*
> *Take a cup and drink it up,*
> *Then call your neighbours in.*

A **crosspatch** was a colloquial term for a <u>cross, ill-tempered person</u> from the 17th century onwards, and used for either a <u>fool</u> or a <u>child</u>. This nursery rhyme suggests two good ways of getting out of the sulks: a soothing occupation such as spinning, then a nice cup of something to drink – tea, coffee, gin, a glass of wine, whatever. After that, you've cheered up enough to get the neighbours in for a patchwork evening or a <u>quilting bee</u>, and the cure is complete.

Incidentally, using the term a <u>bee</u> to mean an <u>informal get-together</u> developed in the USA in the late 18th century. Sometimes it would be arranged to provide for one member of the group, such as making quilts for a girl's dowry. If the term originated in the female companionship of a beehive where all the workers collect honey for the queen bee, it has developed into other types of group activity for either sex, such as <u>spelling bees</u>, as well as <u>quilting and sewing bees</u>.

CUT

The phrase to **have your work cut out** means that you have a clear task before you and much to do; it's easy to see how tailors could face mounting challenges, since it is quicker to cut out a garment than to sew it up. This phrase seems to have first been used in this sense in the mid 19th century in *A Christmas Carol* by Charles Dickens.

We might describe someone as **a cut above the rest**, meaning they are much better than the others in their group. It comes from the superior cut of their tailored clothing but is now used as a general term of approval. There's also a Welsh-English hybrid phrase for this – **he's torri cut** – meaning he's smartly dressed.

If we say to someone, 'I don't think you are **cut out to be** …' say, a surgeon or an astronaut, it means we don't think it's within their natural abilities. They might be very **cut up about it**, meaning upset. We also describe something that has deeply and terribly hurt our feelings as **the unkindest cut of all**, and this metaphorical use of the term has been around since the 16th century.

DISTAFF ☞ SPIN

When you spin with a hand spindle it's hard to hold the raw wool high enough. You need a sort of arm extension, and that's what a distaff is – a stick onto which bunches of soft raw wool are loosely tied. The word itself probably comes from combining <u>staff</u>, meaning a <u>stick</u>, with <u>dizen</u>, meaning to <u>dress</u> in the sense of winding loose wool or flax around it. **The distaff side of the family** describes the female line, defining women still by our long time role as providers of cloth.

DRAB ☞ SURNAME

The three witches in Shakespeare's *Macbeth* include in their nasty potion 'the finger of a birth-strangled babe, ditch-delivered by a drab'. **Drab** now means anything rather dull and boring or lacking colour, either literally or figuratively, but it had quite a number of associations in the past. One was a term for a common prostitute of a very low type, <u>drab</u> perhaps from the poor quality of her dress. When all her charms had departed, she served as midwife or abortionist to desperate women – hence Shakespeare's use of the term.

In the 18th century **drab** described cloth of a rather subdued greyish-brown colour. The religious group known as Quakers, whose dress was always modest, approved of wearing **drab**. The word may have come originally from <u>drape</u>, which was Old French for both <u>undyed cloth</u> and a verb meaning to <u>weave wool into cloth</u>.

Alternatively, the word could have sprung direct from a **draper** – one who <u>deals in cloth</u> – with the commodity taking its name from the purveyor, as do **drapes** and **drapery** for curtains or any loose covering. However, its most direct line connects with the Celts, for whom <u>drab</u> meant <u>hempen</u> or <u>linen cloth of a darkish natural shade</u>, and bequeathed us the modern meaning of <u>a dull, uninteresting colour</u>.

When Shakespeare described a miserable facial expression as, 'These, but the trappings and the Suites of woe,' he was using a textile word from the same source. **Trappings** in this context means <u>decorations</u> or <u>embellishments</u>, and comes from <u>drapes</u>, the <u>d</u> having become a <u>t</u>. <u>Trappings</u> referred to a <u>saddle cloth</u>

or other fabric draped over a horse.

The verb **to drape** was originally only applied to woollen cloth. Today, of course, it still has fabric associations, but not exclusively. A girl might **drape herself affectionately round** some lucky fellow, a rock could be **draped with** seaweed, or a baby may **drape** everything with pasta while learning to feed himself.

DRIZZLING ☞ TANGLE and UNRAVEL

Unpicking the gold and silver thread from old brocades and embroidery to sell for melting down was a dreadful pastime of the rich in the 18th century. Dreadful, that is to say, for the long-term preservation of textiles. It was called <u>parfilage</u>, which bears an obvious link to the French <u>fil</u>, a <u>thread</u>, and became a craze for nearly 50 years at the Court of Versailles. Ladies would carry bags of old textile scraps and implements to unpick them when paying calls or at the theatre.

This pastime spread to England, where it became all the rage, brought by refugees or aristocratic émigrés fleeing the French Revolution. Although the pastime had been carried out to some extent in previous centuries, when it became fashionable among society ladies it attracted the alternative name of <u>drizzling</u>, because the sound made by the stiff, unravelling threads resembled <u>fine rain falling</u>.

The original motive in France was greed rather than economy, although the aristocratic émigrés in England, who had little to sell but their clothes and jewels, presumably needed the money. Tradesmen began to cash in by selling small items as presents from which the precious threads could be drizzled. In France, the practice went out of fashion after the Duc de Chartres was once almost undressed by his admirers as they purloined the trimmings from his coat and pocketed them.

Drizzling lasted somewhat longer in England, and in 1801 there was a burglary in the House of Lords in London in which all the gold lace and other precious metals were stripped from the throne – except, oddly enough, those on the Royal Arms. Perhaps a Royalist burglar with a conscience?

DYED IN THE WOOL ☞ FLEECE, TENTERHOOKS and WOOL

We use the phrase **dyed in the wool** for someone who is a bit set in his ways, rigid and unchangeable. It comes from the practice of dyeing a whole fleece before its wool was spun and made into thread. The dye would go right through all the fibres of the cloth made from that yarn, instead of staying mainly on the surface of the threads.

EENIE MEENIE MINIE MO

There have been a number of theories about the origins of counting out rhymes, of which **eenie meenie minie mo** is among the best known. Druids selecting people for sacrifice may have used them – a dramatic and colourful idea – but it is just as likely that they were employed for counting <u>sheep</u> or counting <u>stitches</u>, and may have had magic significance.

ELASTIC ☞ LEASH

Just think what a lot we owe to elastic. Without it, the wobbly and droopy bits of our figures could only be supported by whalebone stays and tight lacing. In Latin, the word <u>elasticus</u> means something that <u>expands spontaneously</u>, or <u>resumes its normal shape after stretching</u>, and the term has been in the English language since the 17th century. It comes originally from the Latin, <u>laxare</u>, meaning to <u>release</u> or <u>let go</u>. Any loose fabric, such as a knitted or interlocked type, can have <u>elastic properties</u>, but the innovation of incorporating rubber into the threads and cords in the 19th century allowed for much more stretchiness.

We might say of someone that they have **elastic morals** or **an elastic conscience**, meaning a weak or corrupt person with **no moral fibre** who can stretch his or her principles. Presumably, since we are all capable of **stretching the truth** a little at times, we mean that they do this beyond what we consider proper. The courts of law sometimes try to **stretch** a legal definition to cover new ideas, as if it was a piece of elastic.

EMBROIDER ☞ STITCH and SEW

If you accused me of **embroidering the truth**, you would mean that, though not perhaps quite lying, I was certainly adding a good deal of exaggeration and invention to what I was telling you. We embroiderers are a tricksy lot, and might look you straight in the eye and declare that our work literally does embroider the truth.

Anyway, what's wrong with adding decoration, colour and texture to a bare narrative? It makes life much more fun. Embroiderers know that there are many different types of embroidery as well as vast numbers of stitches. Although many of these stitches have interesting and even exotic names, they are all derived from everyday life, and not the other way round. In fact, I cannot think of any that have been used as figures of speech or become idioms in common use. Incidentally, embroidery patterns have a lot in common with tattooing, and Marco Polo described tattoos as 'flesh embroidery'.

Embroidery is an Anglo-Norman word, embrouderie from the verb to embrouder, which is a compound of an earlier base ea for in and brouder, which is probably linked to the past participle of braid, so originally the word meant something braided, from the twisted appearance of the threads in stitching. Among the greatest artistic accomplishments of the Middle Ages are the embroideries collectively called *Opus Anglicanum*, which simply translates as English work.

Embroidery is all about embellishing fabric to make it look beautiful, but because of its fragility, its early history can be deduced more from myths than artefacts. For example, in the Baltic tradition, the sun is female, and as Sol or Saule, is carried across the sky in her golden chariot. She spins precious metals, and embroiders her own dazzling silken clothing all over with gold, silver and bronze threads, removing her dress at night and putting it on again at dawn. She lives on a farm in the sky, and is seen rolling and hopping and dancing in silver shoes on Midsummer morning, which is a time of sexual licence and celebration of life in Baltic culture.

We use embroidering as a figure of speech poetically when we talk of a field as **embroidered with flowers**. Chaucer describes a fine young squire, whose clothes, embellished with floral patterns, seem so much the most important thing about him:

> He was embroidered like a meadow bright,
> And full of freshest flowers, red and white.

Or we can quote Yeats:

> Had I the heavens' embroidered cloths
> Enwrought with golden and silver light...
> I would spread the cloths under your feet.

And no less a poet than John Milton wrote (in *Lycidas*) of 'Every flower that sad embroidery wears'.

So, embroidery can be full of love, laughter and life — quite at odds with some people's view of it today as old-fashioned, dull and prissy. It also has its darker side. Men in particular have always been unsure about how to regard a woman sewing. On the one hand, she is in a submissive pose, eyes down, quiet and passive, probably making something for the home or the children. On the other hand, she is seductive, self-contained and inaccessible in her concentration.

There are tribes in Eastern Siberia who believe that, when women embroider, they are working magic and can ensnare souls in the looping of their thread. The verb, tcagcott means both to embroider a pattern and to cast a spell. Men won't watch women at work, lest the twisting threads disorient them so that they lose their way while hunting.

Even more sinister is the Norse story of how the tragic heroine Gudrun stayed for seven years with Thora, daughter of Hakon of Denmark, after the killing of her husband, the mighty hero Sigurd. She and Thora spent the time making an elaborate embroidery. Judging from Gudrun's history, which is a bloody cycle of disasters and revenge killings, many of them instigated by Gudrun herself, I do not believe that the ladies were indulging in a little light relaxation. More likely, they were pursuing the war by magic means, creating pictures intended to bring about results in the real world, and this idea is enhanced by the mention of seven years, seven being a magic number.

The anonymous poet of the Gudrunarkvida, the saga about Gudrun, has her describing her occupation.

> I sat with Thora for seven seasons,
> Hakon's daughter, in Denmark;
> to give me joy she embroidered in gold
> southern halls and Danish swans.
> We two portrayed the play of warriors,
> the leader's troops with delicate toil,
> red shields and ranks of Huns,
> a sword-band, a helm-band, a leader's train.

Not a lot of laughs in the Norse legends unless, like the Vikings, your idea of something funny is people getting mutilated and killed. A Viking would apparently *laugh himself into stitches* when limbs flew off and blood spurted — so long as the wound wasn't his own.

EXCHEQUER

The chief finance minister for the UK also has cloth connections. **Chancellor of the Exchequer** is a title dating back to the reign of Henry I. In the early 12th century, Henry not only introduced a revolution in medieval accounting, but also died without any debts, which was exceptional for a leader at that, or indeed at any other, time. His method, which was based on use of the Middle Eastern abacus, consisted of laying a checked cloth on a large, oblong counting table with a raised edge. The money to be counted was piled on the different squares of the cloth, and so could be much more easily sorted out and counted.

The cloth was known as **the exchequer** because it resembled a <u>chess board</u>. The original Vulgar Latin <u>scaccus</u> meant a <u>check</u>, or <u>coloured square</u>, which later developed into <u>scaccarium</u>, a chessboard. The term from Old French was <u>eschequier</u>, and that variation arrived with the Norman Conquest to become the Anglo-Norman <u>escheker</u>. By the 14th century the <u>checked cloth</u> was firmly established as the name of the financial department.

So, not only have we inherited **an Exchequer** and its Chancellor from a textile origin, but we also sign **cheques** – or **checks** in the USA – as a form of payment. **Cheque-book journalism** was a phrase coined in the 1960s for the practice of making obscenely large payments to individuals to gain an exclusive story, particularly where this involved rewarding criminals and the corrupt. We regard cheques and banknotes as a simple promissory substitute for coinage, but printing such things on pressed cellulose echoes much earlier times, when, in many parts of the world, cloth itself was used as a form of currency.

Oh, and by the way, the **Chancellor of the Exchequer** kept his money in a **budget**, a word derived from the Old French <u>bouge</u>, meaning both a <u>leather sack</u> and <u>womb</u>. Next time you see the British **Chancellor of the Exchequer** on **Budget Day** waving his big, red **budget box** outside Number 11 Downing Street in London, just think: he is holding up a metaphorical womb, from which all sorts of riches should pour, as from an ancient earth mother or goddess. Remembering where that rubescent case originated may make you feel slightly more cheerful about the hike in the price of petrol or alcohol. Or maybe not.

··· *The Exchequer* *···*

FABRIC ☞ CLOTH, MADE UP OUT OF WHOLE CLOTH, MATERIAL and STUFF

In ancient Rome, a faber was a workman using hard materials such as wood or stone, a term probably derived from a lost word meaning fitting things together. Fabrica, therefore, became the building where the artisan worked, leading to the French word fabrique, which came to us both as fabricate and the body or fabric of a building. Only in the 18th century did the sense of something manufactured produce our present understanding of fabric as a synonym for a textile.

We use the term **the fabric of society** to describe that tenuous but vital network of customs, duties and expectations that bind a culture together. It tends to be used in warning diatribes about anything that might threaten social stability.

Textiles have often been regarded as strikingly dangerous in this respect. For example, many governments have tried to prevent upstart peasants aping their betters, by reserving certain cloths or colours for the upper classes. In ancient China, yellow was reserved for the Emperor alone, and it was treason, punishable by death, for anyone else to wear it. The ancient Greeks forbade women to wear more than three items of clothing, and legislation was passed in 17th century Venice to prevent prostitutes from looking like respectable women.

Similar attempts at control in England resulted in the Sumptuary Laws between about 1350 and 1650, and it has to be said they met with little or no success in reducing conspicuous consumption. The word consumption itself comes from the Latin sumptus, meaning expensive, which came down to us through the Old French somtueux; thus sumptuous came to mean not just costly but lavish and luxurious.

Government is quite right (I hate saying that). What we wear sends very powerful unspoken messages about who we are, or would like to be, and such aspirations and pretensions are often subversive to law and order. When we talk about people wearing distinctive dress, words trip from our tongues loaded with a charge of emotional connections and value judgements. We feel their garments threaten the very **web of life, the material universe** and **the fabric of society**. Unless we're careful, they might even – since I don't see why I can't join in the act of exaggerated metaphor – **unravel the very socks of our existence**.

FAIR TO MIDDLING

Ask an older New Englander 'How are you?' and he or she may reply, 'Oh, *fair to middling*, thanks.' The phrase means <u>not too bad</u> or moderately good, and originated in the American cotton industry. The categories of cotton were <u>Inferior</u>, <u>Fine</u>, <u>Middling</u> and <u>Fair</u>. The first known use of these terms as a figure of speech occurred in a report about the food served at a dinner in Richmond, Virginia, in 1837. By the 1890s, the saying was also noted in England with its current meaning of being so-so – not all that good. Most of the textile mill managers in the USA came from Britain in the 19th and early 20th centuries, so there was a general exchange of textile terms and patois between the two countries.

FAST AND LOOSE ☞ CORD and STRING

There used to be a string game known as *fast and loose*, used by conmen at fairs in 16th century England. The con artist laid string down in a complicated pattern with a stick in the middle. It would appear to the punter that the stick would inevitably catch in the loops of string when it was pulled tight. However this was an optical illusion, and when the mug placed his bet, he inevitably lost his money. The conman had *played fast and loose with him*.

FILIGREE ☞ BEAD

Early beads were often seeds, wood or pieces of stone with a hole through them. The Latin <u>filum</u> for a thread and <u>granum</u> for a seed came together in Italian to form the word <u>filigrana</u>, becoming <u>filigrane</u> in French and *filigree* in English, meaning delicate lacy ornaments made of gold or silver thread and beads. It can now mean any sort of interlaced or pierced work in metal or stone, such as an architectural feature.

FILING CABINET ☞ FILIGREE, FILLET and THREAD

How odd that *filing cabinet* should be a *thread* term, but so it is. It's a very good example of how English draws on varied sources to name thread-like entities. The Latin words <u>filum</u> and <u>filamentum</u>, along with <u>filare</u>, or <u>filure</u>, which is the verb meaning <u>to spin</u>, gave us <u>filament</u> for a thread. A similar word <u>fibre</u> also comes directly from the Latin <u>fibra</u>, and hence the closely linked English word <u>fibre</u>, originally spelt <u>fiber</u> – as it still is in the USA.

The Latin noun _filum_ became _fil_ in Old French. We English speakers laid claim to this word in the specific sense of a string or wire stretched between two points, on which documents and records could be hung for ease of reference – a kind of washing line for clerks. This was certainly a known use in 1525.

By the early 16th century the _filum_ had become something more: a list of documents arranged in a set order. As cupboards and other storage systems developed, we began calling some of them **filing cabinets**, and referred to the compartmentalised documents as **files**. At about the same time, a column of soldiers, or other orderly people in narrow columns started to be described as **in file** or **forming a file**.

The other sort of _file_ for rubbing wood or metal derives from a different root, thought to be the proto-Germanic _fhikala_, whose earliest meaning links it to cutting.

FILLET ☞ FILIGREE, FILING CABINET and THREAD

The word **fillet**, still occasionally used for a thin strip of material, was derived from _filum_, the Latin word for a thread of flax. The sense of a detachable strip has been retained in **a fillet of beef**, or **to fillet a fish** – words far removed from the delicate ribbon _fillets_ with which women in ancient Greece bound up their hair.

FILTER

When ordinary people put everyday objects to some new use, fresh words are born. A simple woollen cloth gave us the word **filter**, which is a Middle English variant of felt from the second half of the 16th century. It came about, of course, because someone used a handy piece of cloth as a strainer to remove any impurities from liquid. This evolved into the hair sieve, whose bottom was made of finely woven hairs or threads. The term has been used for separating off other things, even traffic, which may be allowed into a **filter lane** to speed up the flow.

You make felt by rubbing woollen fibres hard in hot soapy water. Most of us have inadvertently done this to the family socks or sweaters by running too hot a cycle in the washing machine. Here is a myth about the childhood of King Solomon, of later Biblical fame, who one day had a tremendous tantrum. The infant Solomon roared in rage and the hot tears poured down his cheeks, soaking the woollen carpet. He stamped his little feet so hard and long that the woollen rug under him became flattened and strengthened. He had turned it into the first known piece of felt. Since then, felt has been used throughout the Middle East for clothing, tents, saddlebags and everything else imaginable. Solomon had no more tantrums and became known as 'The Wise'.

FLANNEL ☞ COTTON and WOOL

Flannel as we know it is a strong cotton fabric with a long, <u>plush nap</u>. *To flannel* someone is to flatter them, presumably because you can stroke the cloth in the same way as you stroke your rich uncle, boss, or other person when you want to please them. Be careful, though. In North America a *flannelmouth* is a poisonous snake, so not everything to do with fabric should be caressed, and even rich uncles and bosses, when *flannelled*, have been known to turn and bite.

The word <u>flannel</u> is an English corruption of the Welsh <u>gwlannen</u> or <u>gwlân</u>, meaning wool, and seemingly related to the Czech <u>vlna</u>. Perversely, the English used the word for a cotton fabric, while the Welsh kept it for a <u>loose-textured woollen stuff</u>.

Shakespeare used *flannel* in *The Merry Wives of Windsor* as a jocular name for a Welshman, and some Welsh towns, such as Abergavenny, still have a *flannel street*, commemorating what was once a very important manufacture. A surprising use for good Welsh flannel was to boil it with sugar and add it to a mixture of lime and ox blood. This made a very strong sealant, and was used in 1805 to join together the cast-iron sections of the Pontcysyllte aqueduct in Wales, UK. The aqueduct is still watertight and still carrying boats along the Llangollen Canal. There's nice!

FLAX ☞ LINEN and TOW

If it's true that gentlemen prefer blondes, then the *flaxen-haired* beauties of fairy tales were probably popular with the opposite sex. Flax is thread made from the fibres of the flax or linen plant, *Linum ussitatissimum*, and when it has been treated and bound onto a distaff for spinning, it looks like long, blonde locks of hair. We therefore describe blonde youths or women as *flaxen-haired* or *tow-haired*, because fair hair looks like the yellowish-white or silvery colours of the best quality flax fibres. In the USA a light-haired child is still referred to as *tow-headed* or a *tow-head*, especially in the Southern states. <u>Flax thread</u> is also known as <u>straw</u>, which illuminates the meaning of those fairy tales where the heroine has to spin straw into gold.

There are lots of stories and superstitions about the flax plant. One says that it can be bleached to the most beautiful silvery-white by laying it out in the light of the moon. Strange as it sounds, there may be some truth in this, as the best bleaching comes when there is dew at dawn to wet the flax, which is then left out through a day of sunshine – and these are often the exact weather conditions that follow a clear, moonlit night.

Once, so the story goes, a beautiful flaxen-haired girl was due to wed a handsome Prince. She was rich and spoiled and too lazy to spin. When the threads of flax tangled, she couldn't be bothered to unwind them, so she tossed them on the floor. Her young serving girl collected up the threads, unravelled the snarls, spun and wove them into a magnificent wedding dress. So the Prince married her instead. Hooray!

FLEECE ☞ BAA BAA BLACK SHEEP and WOOL

The entire coat of wool, taken off in one piece – most extremely with the hide – is known as the <u>fleece</u>, which probably comes from the Latin <u>pluma</u>. This originally meant <u>down</u>, the fluffy undercoat of birds, and later <u>feathers</u>.

<u>Pluma</u> doesn't sound much like <u>fleece</u>, but that is due to something that word experts call the 'Germanic Sound Shift'. I know that sounds like a highly-starched crackly undergarment, but it's really only an observation that many words beginning with '<u>p</u>' in Latin changed to '<u>f</u>' in the Germanic languages. These include the Scandinavian, Icelandic and Dutch languages, as well as German and English. We probably derived fleece from some intermediate words, such as the old Germanic <u>fleusa</u>, via one of these other countries.

To *fleece someone* is to take all their money, or every bit of whatever else they have. The idea of <u>robbing heartlessly</u> comes fairly obviously from the idea of stripping or shearing a helpless sheep, and was first noted in the late 16th century.

I am sure Esau, the older twin born to Isaac and Rebekah, felt he had been properly *fleeced*. He is described in the Bible as 'a hairy man' and his father's favourite, while Rebekah doted on Jacob, who managed with her help to cheat brother Esau out of his most precious inheritance, his father's official blessing. We are told that old Isaac had become blind, but wanted to give his blessing to his elder son before he died. Jacob's mother Rebekah made a meal from the flesh of young goats, then bound their soft kidskin onto Jacob's arms and the back of his neck, so that Isaac was fooled by touch into giving his irreplaceable blessing to the younger twin.

One of the oldest breeds of sheep is the Jacob's sheep, recalling the Biblical conman. They are piebald, bear up to six horns, and may have originated in the Middle East.

In Western Europe, we are more accustomed to white sheep. Anything soft and white, like a cloud or snow, can therefore be described as **fleecy**, and wool is often used as a standard for whiteness. Although most sheep are off-white, and many are streaky or black, we have it on the good authority of a nursery rhyme that:

> Mary had a little lamb,
> Its fleece was white as snow;
> And everywhere that Mary went,
> The lamb was sure to go.

The fleece from Mary's lamb was, of course, **lamb's-wool**, which is also the name of a type of punch popular in 17th century England. One old recipe describes mixing the pulp of half a dozen roasted apples with raw sugar, grated nutmeg and a little ginger and adding it to a quart [roughly a litre] of strong ale, slightly warmed. This can be served warm in a bowl, with sweet cakes floating on the top. It'll warm the cockles of your heart, but I'm not sure you'd get much spinning done after it.

Putting out a fleece is also a phrase that comes from the Bible. Gideon believed he had a mission to rescue the people of Israel. To test whether he had interpreted God's instructions correctly, he laid fleece out on the ground and prayed. He asked that in the morning, the fleece would be wet, and the surrounding ground dry. This took place but, still unsure, Gideon asked that the opposite should also happen. Next morning, sure enough, the ground was wet but the fleece was dry. So **to put out a fleece** suggests asking for guidance but being prepared to verify the answer in some way.

The fleece holds a special place in Classical Greek mythology. Jason and his companions, the Argonauts, were sent to seek the miraculous Golden Fleece, which hung from a tree in Colchis on the Black Sea, guarded by a never-sleeping dragon. Jason eventually succeeded in stealing it, after many strange adventures.

To speak of a **golden fleece** suggests something fabulously expensive and gained at great personal price. It is thought that there may even have been some truth in the legend, since the early people of Colchis were said to collect gold dust from underground rivers and mines by dredging with fleeces, probably the hide of a skinned animal with its wool on. The precious metal would have been caught and held by the wool, making the fleece glitter with gold.

Let's finish on a happy note, with a nursery rhyme about fleecing, or shearing, a sheep that delightfully catches our tendency to selective deafness.

> Old woman, old woman, shall we go a-shearing?
> Speak a little louder, sir, I'm very thick of hearing.
> Old woman, old woman, shall I love you dearly?
> Thank you very kindly, sir, now I hear you clearly

FLOCK ☞ FLEECE and FLUFFY

I'm not sure if we can count <u>flock</u> as a textile word, though it must have acquired its sheep connections very early. The Latin <u>floccus</u> meant a <u>lock</u> or <u>tuft</u>, particularly of <u>wool</u>, a meaning that remains in terms such as a <u>flock mattress</u> to mean one stuffed with wool waste. In posh language we can also describe things that are <u>soft and fluffy</u> as <u>flocculent</u>, from the same source. But the dictionary says that the word, a <u>flock</u>, to describe a group of people or animals comes from an unknown origin. The Latin <u>floccus</u> seems to have given rise to <u>vlocke</u>, <u>flokkr</u>, <u>floke</u> or <u>flocc</u> for a tuft in Old English. Surely the compiler must have noticed how a sheep appears to be covered in lots of identical locks of flokes – flocks and flocks of floccus, in fact. Maybe, if we **flock together** no one will dare say we are wrong.

FLUFFY ☞ FLEECE and FLOCK

So many things to do with thread are said to be <u>fluffy</u> that you might think it has always been a textile word. Funnily enough, it wasn't originally. The word <u>fluff</u> is of unknown origin, possibly a dialect version of <u>flue</u>, to do with puffing away a wisp of <u>smoke</u>. Thread can be spun from anything soft – thistledown, the downy undercoat of birds and animals, human hair, fur from the family pet – as well as cotton, silk, flax and wool. All these things can be described as **fluffy**. The word has lost its link with <u>smoke</u> and established a much happier liaison with all sorts of textiles.

The word is also used metaphorically for this quality of soft puffiness. However, calling a young woman *a bit of fluff* could be regarded as patronising. We describe *fluffing a task* as failing at it, and actors are said *to fluff their lines* when they forget what they were meant to say. *Fluffing* is also slang for farting.

Fluffers or *fluffies* was a descriptive term for the women who cleaned up the hair and dust on the Tube (the London Underground) at night when the trains stopped running. Perhaps because we *fluff* up cushions when tidying the sitting room, *fluffers* are also people who prepare a house for sale, making it look its best, and the same term is used for the warm-up act before the star attraction in a show. Take care who you refer to as a *fluffer* though, as the term is also used in the porn industry for a woman hired to excite the male member – pun intended – to get him sexually ready for the action shots.

FOLLOWING A THREAD ☞ BALL OF THREAD and CLUE

This is a very common metaphor for any journey or search, and usually suggests trying to follow a difficult, slightly obscure path, requiring care and attention to details. It is often used as a figure of speech to suggest development of ideas or actions according to a theme or common element that links them all.

The Ariadne story, mentioned in the entry for **clue**, is probably the earliest version of this journey in Western literature. *Following a thread* became a motif in many other stories, which developed their own distinctive flavour. Here's a Celtic tale that illustrates why this particular symbol has such a hold on us.

In the traditional Celtic story, *The Island of Women*, the hero, Bran, son of Febal, makes a voyage and comes to an island where he sees a beautiful woman on the shore. She throws him a ball of thread and winds him, and his ship, into port. She is the queen of an island of delights, where he and his men each find a partner, relax in a luxurious palace and enjoy wonderful food. After a year, one man becomes very homesick and persuades the company to leave, but when they reach the homeland, no one recognises them, except from old tales. Only a year has passed for the enchanted sailors, but in the real world, hundreds of years have passed. When the homesick man leaps ashore, he turns to dust. Bran sets sail again, and he and his company are said to be sadly searching for the island and the lovers they lost, until this very day.

FRAY ☞ WEAR

If you annoy me enough, I might say I feel **frayed around the edges**, or that **my nerves and my temper are frayed**. Fray in this sense comes from the Latin fricare, to rub, from which we get friction, and I suppose being rubbed up the wrong way. It's from a different source from fray meaning battle.

FRAZZLED ☞ WEAR

One of the most evocative textile phrases we still employ is **I'm worn to a frazzle**. This probably comes from combining fray with fazzle, a dialect word for tangle. However, another suggestion is that to frazzle was an American verb meaning to tear to ribbons. It appeared in one of the popular Uncle Remus stories about Brer Rabbit in 1881, and has since been generally adopted.

FRINGE ☞ WEAVE

When you finish a piece of weaving what do you do with the long warp threads left on the end? Two ways are obvious. You can weave them back into the fabric with a needle, or you can tie them in little bundles to leave an ornamental fringe. Extra weft thread can also be left at the sides of the cloth for the same purpose, and beads or other ornaments added.

The word fringe comes directly from the Latin fimbria, meaning a thread. A **fringe event** is therefore a textile figure of speech for something peripheral to the main activities, such as **fringe theatre** or **fringe benefits**, which are perks on the side, and not part of the usual remuneration.

Left-over warp and weft threads could also be tied in tassels, and these very decorative devices are used on their own to ornament all sorts of things, including clothing. The word came from the Latin tassa, a clasp, as tassels were used in the Middle Ages to fasten cloaks by pulling them through a metal ornament. Tassels had many other uses, and many symbolic and magic associations. **Tassel** is also used as slang for the male genitalia.

FUSTIAN ☞ BOMBASTIC, SHODDY and SLEAZY

What is it about cloth that makes us use it in a derogatory way about people? Fustian is a coarse cloth that takes its name from Fostat, a suburb of Cairo, Egypt. Since the 16th century **talking fustian** has signified inflated, pompous, bombastic speech, or using too much jargon.

··· *Grasp the Nettle* ···

GRASP THE NETTLE ☞ SPIN

Material for spinning needn't always be fluffy; any reasonably pliable fibres will do. A strong and serviceable fibre can be spun from nettles, so those fairytales where the heroine has to gather nettles with her bare hands and spin, weave and sew a magic shirt are not so fanciful after all.

Nettles are used for food as well as spinning, and you don't get stung so long as you pick them by grasping and holding them very firmly. Then the hairs, which are soft, bend harmlessly instead of pricking your skin. We use this figure of speech, **grasping the nettle**, to indicate getting a firm and decisive grip on a situation.

To nettle someone is to annoy them, as if with the stinging irritation of a nettle, and urticaria or **nettle rash** is a red raised rash on the skin that resembles nettle stings, but is caused by heat or allergy.

GROGGY

We might say we are **feeling groggy** if we are a bit muzzy or unwell, but it originally meant the worse for drink. That's thanks to an 18th century Admiral of the British fleet, who ordered the crew's ration of rum to be watered down – hence grog. But why was Admiral Vernon known as **old groggy**? It was because he wore a coat of grogram, and the sailors derisively applied the nickname to the drink, and later to its befuddling effects.

Grogram came from the French gros grain or coarse grain, which was a rough cloth of a silk and wool or mohair mix, stiffened with gum. Coats were made of this fabric from the 16th to the 19th century. Today, especially in America, grosgrain means a horizontally ribbed ribbon, used as a trim, as a support for buttons and buttonholes on the edge of a jumper or cardigan.

HACKLE ☞ FLAX

Another implement used to comb or card fibres for spinning is the heckle or hackle which has iron spikes hammered into a wooden back, like a comb. The word hackle seems to have come originally from hacile, a Latin word for a cloak, via other words for a garment or covering, which would seem to be jumping ahead to the end result. By the 15th century one meaning for the word was a comb for splitting the fibres of flax and hemp.

The hackles are also the fur round a dog's neck or the stiff neck feathers of a game bird, perhaps because they stand up in spikes when the creature is angry or frightened. Hence **to get your hackles up** means to prepare for a fight.

Hackles made of feathers are worn on the hats of some British army regiments, usually pinned in place by the cap badge. The Black Watch battalion of the Royal Regiment of Scotland wear their famous **red hackle**, while soldiers of the Royal Welsh Regiment wear a **white hackle**, in honour of the Prince of Wales and the three ostrich feathers that form his badge.

In the early 17th century, an instrument for beating flax, now obsolete, was the tewtaw, and its action was known as heckling. One wonders at the similarity to the tawse, a Scottish dialect word for a whip with many thongs, used to discipline children. Both taw and thew have meanings relating to beating things, and people, into better order. There seem to be a lot of linked words around these processes partly because of dialect variations. **Heckle** in some places has the added meaning of catechising someone severely to test out their weak spots.

In other places, a heck is a hatch or grating in a river, sieving fish from the water, so maybe that is how it came to mean a sifting out or sieving of a person. The audience may **heckle** a speaker or performer by calling out to upset him, presumably with a similar sense of testing.

A heckle was also the word used for something that guided threads through a reel in both spinning and weaving. This heckle has an obvious similarity of purpose to the heddle, which is a kind of grid or comb made of wires and loops through which the warp threads are passed alternately, allowing the weft thread to go through easily when the heddle is raised.

Confusing? Yes, because a completely different etymology could come from hack, which means both a hatch or grid and a tool for chopping or hammering things, as well as the action of bashing something hard or hacking pieces out of it. In Old High German hak meant to pierce, prick or stab, linking to hook. At this stage, let's remind ourselves that our language is a fluid, slippery thing, where words may have more than one source and the **threads** may get crossed and tangled.

Hack as a word for a broken-down old horse or a broken-down old journalist has nothing to do with either meaning of hack. It has been used since the 13th century for an ordinary riding horse or nag for hire, or men or women as drudges. One suggestion is that the term derived from the village of Hackney, now part of London, where horses for the carriage trade — hackney cabs — were bred for renting out.

By heck as an exclamation has nothing to do with any of the above, but is probably a slightly disguised rendering of 'By Hell!' originally from Lancashire in the UK, where the men folk wear flat caps, keep ferrets down their trousers and get to say 'Eee, there's trouble at t'mill,' — at least that's the outsiders' view of them.

HANK ☞ BALL OF THREAD and SKEIN

Threads can be wound into a hank, a word in use since the 16th century, and probably derived from an earlier word, now lost, denoting to clasp or to suspend — hence **hanging** something or someone. The Old Norse hanku could be a string coil, band or the ear of a pot, bequeathing us **handle** and **to handle**. It could also suggest suspension, in the metaphoric sense of **hanging about**, and **hanker**, denoting a craving, longing or yearning, as in **I hanker after a pair of red shoes**.

HEM ☞ SEAM and SEW

Seaming and hemming are among the more routine tasks of sewing. The word hem, which now means the folding over and stitching of an edging on fabric, came originally from hemme, Old Frisian for enclosed land. It is linked with ham, which is still a component of many village and town names, such as Birmingham, Sydenham, Ham, and the word hamlet itself.

The word hem has been used in sewing since the 15th century or before; related figures of speech often go back to the earlier, land-related, sense. To be **hemmed in** is to be surrounded, and usually carries negative feelings. You might be **hemmed in by the enemy** or **hemmed in by cares**, though that suggests a surreal picture of being carefully sewn into the edge of a garment.

HEMP ☞ FLAX and LINEN

What a pretty show that annual plant Cannabis sativa makes in your herbaceous border. The only trouble is that you will shortly receive a visit from the police, as the growing of any variety of **hemp** is still illegal except under special government licence. This is because some people still believe it can only be used for the production of the illegal drug, marijuana. As a textile enthusiast you are growing it for its very strong and useful fibres. (I do believe you, honestly I do.)

Hemp has been grown in the Far East for 5,000 years or more and was probably used to produce fibres for clothing in Europe from the 5th century AD. Very few varieties can be used to produce marijuana; most are useful for the seeds and fibres. These varieties will, deservedly, make a comeback when the hysteria dies down.

Both the words hemp and cannabis originate from the same root. An unknown word from earliest time became kanab in Persian, and xanapiz in Greek, from which we get cannabis. Meanwhile, the proto-Germanic version was something like khanapiz, and became worn down to hanf in German, hennep in Dutch, hamp in Danish, and so to our hemp.

In the Middle Ages, ropes – particularly those used for hanging people – were often made of hemp fibre, so any reference to a **hempen rope** strongly suggested a condemned man.

Later on, the term **hempen** often referred to a rustic, uncouth person, as when Puck in Shakespeare's *A Midsummer Night's Dream* describes some bumpkins as **hempen homespuns**. Hemp fibres also gave us strong textiles on which to paint pictures, and to make tents, and the word **canvas** is also derived from the Greek xanapiz.

INKLING ☞ RED TAPE and TAPED

Here is a word that hints at a whole vanished world. Inkle-weavers were the craftsmen who made – surprise, surprise – inkles. These narrow linen tapes were in huge demand, in all sorts of sizes and for all sorts of purposes, before easier means of fastening were devised. Just think of those unsatisfactory tapes used to tie hospital gowns at the back, revealing so much we'd rather hide.

There is an old saying, **as thick as inkle-weavers**, that for some reason means a group of people who get on very well with each other. The word inkle is of uncertain origin, but may originally be Dutch. It has been recorded since the mid

16th century under various different spellings, including <u>ynchull</u>, <u>ynkell</u>, <u>inckle</u> and <u>incle</u>. The word carried the idea of a <u>hint</u> or a <u>whisper</u> – perhaps a fanciful link because tapes and drawstrings are usually narrower than ribbons – and we say *I haven't an inkling*, to mean <u>I have no idea</u>.

In the 20th century, a small group of Oxford dons, including the writers C.S. Lewis and J.R.R. Tolkien among others, called themselves **The Inklings**. They seem to have chosen the name for its punning connection with ink.

JACQUARD LOOM ☞ LOOM, WEAVE and WEB

The <u>Jacquard loom</u> gave us one of textiles' most significant changes to our way of life and links us directly to the amazing computer technology we have today. An 18th century Frenchman, Joseph-Marie Jacquard, designed a new type of loom for the silk industry, using a series of punched cards that gave coded instructions to the machine. These looms were capable of creating an almost infinite variety of patterns without human skill or intervention. The French Revolution interrupted his work but his invention spread gradually through Europe in the first 30 years of the 19th century.

A heddle on a loom works on the <u>binary system</u>, because it has only two choices – <u>up or down</u> – and a hole punched in a card works in the same way, the two choices being <u>open or closed</u>.

Keep reading … this is important, and easy to understand.

For those not clear about what a binary system is, we normally count using a <u>decimal system</u> of 10 digits, because it comes more naturally to us, as we have the original <u>digits</u> or <u>fingers</u> to hand, as you might say. However, it's more logical and simple for <u>electrical</u> or <u>mechanical devices</u> (such as looms and computers) to work on the <u>binary system</u> with only two digits (1 and 0) representing <u>on and off</u> or <u>charged and uncharged</u> or <u>open and closed</u>.

Jacquard's genius anticipated the use of punched cards to carry computer programs by almost two centuries. This innovation put a lot of skilled textile workers out to grass, as automation often does.

Jacquard's cards paved the way for Charles Babbage's Analytical Engine, a 19th century precursor of the first programmable computer. Once Ada Lovelace, a brilliant female mathematician, had written its first program, the binary system was ready to be used – eventually – in modern digital technology.

This book is an ancient Hindu text, widely considered to be a classic among works on human sexual behaviour, showing techniques and positions for lovemaking. In Sanskrit literature, a holy text is called a <u>sutra</u>. The **Kama Sutra** takes its name from the word for <u>thread</u> or <u>string</u>, and is also linked to <u>siwan</u>, meaning <u>to sew</u>, because early books were written not on paper but on 'pages' of dried leaves sewn together. These proved too fragile and were replaced by thin sheets of wood with holes punched in the edges to allow for fastening with silken thread. We still refer to the <u>leaves</u> of a book. Ye shall read what you sew.

KEMP

There are some words that you didn't know you needed until you hear them and then you can't do without them. How, for example, can you describe those occasional straggly, coarse hairs that stick out of someone's eyebrows or moustache? They are **kemp**, that's what they are, and the job of a woman known as a **kempster** was to pull out such wiry bits from an animal's pelt to leave only the softer, undercoat hairs.

The word <u>kemp</u> comes from Old English <u>cemban</u>, which gives us the verb **to comb**, as in disentangling and straightening hair. It also spawned the no-longer-used **kempt** for combed or tidy, and the still current **unkempt**, meaning untidy and dishevelled. Such negative gibes endure through the ages, while more positive phrases often fade away. It goes to show that we enjoy the discomfiture of others and prefer cutting our rivals down to size rather than praising them.

The '<u>ster</u>' word ending was commonly used for female workers, for example <u>brewster</u> and <u>maltster</u>, and I'm afraid a <u>kempster</u> was fairly low in the hierarchy of medieval peasants. However, wool-combers did have their own patron saint. He was an Armenian Christian called Blaise, torn to pieces by iron combs in 316 AD. On his way to execution he miraculously saved the life of a child who was choking to death, so he is also the saint of sore throat sufferers.

Many wool towns claimed St Blaise as the patron saint for all wool workers and traders, and celebrated his day with feasts and pageants. Women were not supposed to spin during the celebrations and, in the countryside, anyone who was caught spinning on 'Saint Blaze, his day' was likely to have her distaff taken away and burned by her neighbours.

The idea that the saint gave his name to the <u>blazer</u> as an article of clothing is almost certainly fanciful. The jacket came about much later and was named for its bright fiery red colour at St Margaret's College, Oxford. Anyway, St Blaise wasn't burned, even if the workaholics' distaffs were.

KNIT ☞ KNOT, NET and PLAIT

Imagine this scene: a patrol cop is chasing a speeding car. With difficulty, he catches up, pulls alongside, and to his surprise sees a little old lady knitting at the wheel. She pays no attention to his siren and flashing lights, so he rolls down his window and yells, 'Pull over!' She looks up and responds politely, 'No, it's a scarf!'

Knitting is a very ancient textile art but was only brought to Western Europe in medieval times. The etymology of the craft is complicated. <u>Knit</u> and <u>knot</u> are obviously similar in sound and spelling, with both having a sense of twining strands together. Both come from the early Germanic word <u>knudn</u>, meaning a <u>round lump</u>. Knitting doesn't involve making knots directly, although the way the wool is twisted and looped by the needles creates a fabric that looks rather like a <u>net</u>. The practice of knitting became widespread in the first half of the 16th century. It was particularly useful for clothes that needed stretchiness, such as bonnets and stockings. To <u>knot</u> as a verb came in at about this time, and to <u>knit</u> stayed; however, referring to the end product or work in progress as <u>knitting</u> only started in the 18th century.

The earliest known piece of knitting comes from Syria. It was made in handspun wool, and dated to about 250 AD by Yale University. There are medieval paintings of the Virgin Mary knitting, sometimes called the **knitting madonnas**. In one she is shown knitting a sweater for the child Jesus. She is working on four needles, and is just shaping the neck. What's more, there are at least two threads of wool showing, so she is knitting in a pattern, similar to Fair Isle.

There are too many famous knitters in history to roll call them all, but let's remember the sinister <u>tricoteuses</u>: old women who, during the French Revolution, sat by the guillotine counting the numbers of heads rolling into the basket, along with their stitches. The 'Terrible Knitters of Dent' were not sinister at all, however. In Dent in Yorkshire, both men and women knitted so fast that the needles would become hot from the friction. So proficient were they, that many could walk to market, knitting a sock each way, with one knitting needle stuck into a holder in their belts, leaving a hand free to carry their purchases.

A friend told me that she had met an old man in South Wales some 20 years ago, who was knitting straight from a <u>rolag</u> – that is, a tuft of raw unspun wool – which he held under one arm, twisting a thread from it with his fingers. He was knitting on 'needles' made from the long flight feathers of a seagull's wing. I presume he had taken them off the bird first, though, if not, it suggests an even more interesting picture.

In fact, it's possible to knit using anything vaguely stick-like for needles and it certainly can be done with feathers. Apparently in the Shetland Islands of Scotland, the young girls of yesteryear were given the primary feathers from gulls, stripped of their fluffy bits, on which to learn how to knit the amazingly fine Shetland shawls in single-ply wool. This helped the youngsters learn to keep the right degree of tension, as the hollow 'needles' collapse if gripped too tightly. The islanders create beautiful and elaborate patterns in their 'wedding ring' shawls, so called because the finest of them can be drawn through a wedding ring.

The women of the Aran Islands, in Galway Bay, to the west of mainland Ireland, knit **aran sweaters**. They are made of special thick, tough wool, in natural colours and enriched with seemingly embossed designs. Different villages have particular patterns, but the women knit inventive individual motifs as well.

There is a story that these family patterns were created for the sad but practical purpose of being able to identify a man whose body might be washed up after weeks at sea. The story is an appealing one, but almost certainly false. The playwright J. M. Synge used the dramatic device of having a woman identify the body of her drowned brother because of a dropped stitch in his stockings in his play Riders To the Sea, and on that slender basis the idea of a widespread practice took root.

We demonstrate the closeness of knitting and knotting when we say **'This fracture is knitting'** to describe the healing of a bone or a wound. This turn of phrase comes from the same origin as <u>knot</u> and describes the lumpy appearance or feel of the tissues as they heal.

Perhaps, in the same way, **knitting my brows** or **knitting my forehead**, used to describe frowning, may refer to the little lumps of muscle that appear as a result of a look of concentration or concern. This makes more sense than the idea of a piece of knitting being made out of eyebrows, no matter how unkempt.

We speak of a **close-knit** family meaning one that is emotionally close or shows great solidarity. (Perhaps you could knit one from eyebrow hair?)

Finally, for all knit wits – what do you get if you cross a sheep with a kangaroo?

Answer: A little woolly jumper.

KNOT ☞ KNIT

The root of **knot** is just the same as knit, from the proto-Germanic word <u>knudn</u>, meaning a <u>round lump</u>. Its origin may have been more agricultural than textile, as it has bequeathed us the word <u>knoll</u> for a <u>small hill</u>, by way of <u>knolle</u>, a <u>clod</u> or a <u>turnip</u>.

Such a useful word must have attached itself quickly to all sorts of other things. A <u>knop</u> is an archaic word for a <u>button</u>, which later changed into a <u>knob</u>. Similarly a <u>knop</u> is the round <u>blob</u> on the stem of a drinking glass. The related word <u>knuckle</u> applied itself to the <u>protuberances formed by joints on digits</u>. Not least of the word's uses was to describe the <u>lump made by tying a knot</u>. Since the Middle Ages, any protuberance or excrescence that resembles a <u>knotted cord</u> has been described as a <u>knot</u>, such as a healing bone fracture, a tumour, pimple or wart, a bud or an ornamental boss. Textile words certainly get around.

The Old English <u>cnotta</u> meant an <u>intertwining</u> of the parts of one or more ropes or cords, for the purpose of <u>fastening them together</u> or to something else, and then <u>drawing them tight</u>. Words that originally started with a c often ended up in English with a silent <u>k</u>. It's illogical, infuriating to foreigners, and separates all sorts of words which would otherwise appear to go together, including knotting, knitting and netting. The majority of our words came, in the distant past, from the classical languages Latin, Sanskrit and Greek and lots of things happened to them as they drifted and shifted, travelling forwards in time and sideways across continents. We find that often 't' became 'th', and 'k' or 'c' became 'h'. Bear with me if some of the derivations seem far-fetched; they're all in proper reference books.

Muscles can feel as if they have been **knotted** when in spasm, with a perceptible lump under the skin. A **knot** of wood falling out of place has caused the **knothole** in a tree or a worked wooden item, and **knotgrass** has a beaded, grassy stem with a knotty appearance.

To say to someone **Get knotted!** is distinctly odd, but may suggest that you will bring them up in lumps or protuberances if they don't go away and stop bothering you, or at least tie their bodies (or some particular part) in anatomically impossible knots, as in a cartoon fight.

Maybe it refers to the ferocious Russian scourge, known as a **knout**, often fatal in its effects, or the heavy wooden club of the same name.

Knot gardens are laid out in intricate designs with herbs, flowers and small bushes to define the pattern, a **knot** being the word used for a small bunch or posy of flowers. This may be either because it is a small, irregular cluster or, more likely, from the knot or bow of ribbon with which it is tied.

Have you ever wondered why children sing, 'Here we go gathering nuts in May'? It's pretty strange, considering nuts only ripen in the autumn. But this children's dance game once referred to **Knots in May**, a **knot** in this connection meaning the little bunch of flowers. The whole village would be up early on May Day, and sally forth to gather branches of may flowers and little posies of primroses, returning home to dance on the village green, in celebration of spring, in peace and harmony.

That's the theory anyway. If the Puritan preachers were to be believed, these feast days were simply an excuse for everyone to go out, get drunk and have sex. The maypole was pretty obviously a huge phallic symbol, and ancient pagan rites of spring were not acceptable to strait-laced Protestants. Nothing much has changed except that such mad frolics seem to happen more often than once a year for today's youth.

Let's cool our overheated imaginations by a trip on the water. The speed of a boat is still described in **knots per hour**. This figure of speech derives from the old method of measuring the speed of a sailing ship by means of a piece of cord with knots tied in it at intervals. This was trailed behind the boat attached to the logline and timed by a sandglass, to determine the number of nautical miles per hour that the vessel was travelling. If someone gets through their work or anything else fast, you might say they were **going at a fair rate of knots**.

When a typical comedy or detective story reaches the climax of its complicated plot and suddenly everything is revealed, hero and heroine are united, murderers and other assorted villains exposed, and all the world is put to rights again, we exclaim **What a dénoument!** This is an exuberantly French way of saying an <u>unknotting</u> or <u>unravelling</u>, because there's no exact equivalent to the noun in English. Such excessive excitement is usually associated with foreigners, rather than with the buttoned-up and reserved British.

A **knotty problem** is one that is difficult to solve, and it seems as if you will never manage it, unless perhaps someone tells you **to cut the Gordian Knot**, as a way of suggesting you work out a bold and direct solution. The story comes from Classical Greek legend.

Once, in an ancient land called Phrygia, a part of Greece, there was a king called Gordias. Before he was chosen to be king, he had been a peasant. In order to give due praise to the gods and gratitude for his new fortune, he dedicated his old farm cart to Jupiter, and tied the yoke at its front to a beam in his great hall with a knot so complicated and elaborate that no one was able to untie it. Many tried over the years: they were eager to succeed, because a priest had predicted that whoever could undo the knot would rule the whole of Asia – the farthest reaches of the known world.

About 400 years later, along came young Alexander, eventually known as 'The Great'. He listened to the legend, studied the knot carefully, then took out his sword, and in one smooth stroke, cut straight through it. Alexander was only 30 years old when he died, weeping, because there was no more of the world left to conquer. Wise men said that, in cutting the Gordian knot, he had cut short his own life thread.

LACE ☞ TAWDRY

The Latin word for a net is <u>lacis</u> from which we derive the word <u>lace</u>. Intriguingly, the term did not relate directly to thread but instead carried the idea of <u>enticement</u> or <u>entrapment</u>, as with a <u>noose</u> or <u>snare</u>. Of course, those would also have been made of thread, leather thongs or wire.

Thanks to the French <u>laz</u> or <u>las</u>, by the 16th century, <u>lace</u> had come to mean an <u>open fabric made of threads</u>, and the old link with a noose was lost. Still later, English borrowed <u>lazo</u>, the equivalent word for a <u>noose</u> in Spanish, and from this we derived a **lasso** to rope in a herd of animals.

Lace makers in the UK had their own medieval guild and their own patron saint, St Catherine. She was said to have been a beautiful woman of Alexandria, who died in 310 AD. She was martyred for refusing to give up her Christian faith, and is always pictured holding a small wheel, because she was broken on such an instrument of torture. Even today we still remember her, through the whirling firework called a Catherine Wheel, a style of rose stained glass window and a wheel pattern in lace making.

When King Henry VIII imprisoned his first wife, Queen Katherine of Aragon, at Ampthill in Bedfordshire, prior to divorcing her, she discovered the poverty of the local lace makers. The good-hearted Queen burnt all her lace trimmings and commissioned new ones.

In years gone by, both young men and girls were apprenticed as lace makers, and adopted Catherine as their own saint. Celebrations on her day continued until the 19th century, and the apprentices played a game of jumping over a candle flame, still remembered in the nursery rhyme

> Jack be nimble, Jack be quick,
> Jack jump over the candle stick.

Along with lace, the Vulgar Latin lacium gave us both delicious and elicit. That seems very appropriate, given that many men have feared women's ability to make ourselves **look delicious** in order to **elicit** a response, and to **snare** and **lasso** them.

We describe something as **lacy** or **lacey** when it is light and full of holes or spaces. **Lacing up** garments by threading a cord through opposing holes followed on from lace as a fabric, and also gave us the concept of a **latch** to fasten a door. Apparently **to lace into someone** is slang for attacking them, verbally or physically. Could it mean something like to punch them full of holes? Or does it describe the pattern of stripes left by a flogging? To **lace** someone's drink means to add something to it – usually either alcohol or a drug.

If you were on a sailing ship you might admire the **lace-piece**, which is the curved decorative carving behind the figurehead.

LAP DANCER

Surprisingly, the word <u>lap</u> probably comes to us from another early textile word. The Germanic source was <u>lappen</u>, a <u>rag</u> or piece of <u>cloth</u> that formed the <u>flap of a garment</u>, and this probably became **label** via **lobe** in the 14th century.

In Middle English, <u>lap</u> was a verb meaning to <u>wrap</u>, and hence to <u>extend beyond</u>. In the 18th century this gave us **overlap** and the noun **lap** for the <u>space created along one's thighs when seated</u>. The modern meaning of <u>one circuit of a course</u> as a **lap** emerged in the 19th century. However, <u>lap</u> meaning to <u>lick up</u> is from a different source entirely, although a **lap dog** is a small pet that can sit on your lap, and lap up your affection.

Lap dancing is a modern form of entertainment in night clubs, where the erotic dancer sits on a man's <u>lap</u> while he stuffs money into her bra, and it got your attention better than **lap** on its own, didn't it?

LEASH ☞ ELASTIC

A <u>lash</u> was the flexible part of a whip, and so lent itself to the action of <u>lashing</u> someone. Equally, flexible fibres could be used for <u>lashing</u> an object such as a blade or an arrow onto a shaft. In the 16th century this word gave rise to <u>leash</u>, both as an action of <u>tying things together</u> and in the sense of <u>whipping with a cord</u>.

It was only a small step from this to the use of <u>leash</u> as something to <u>restrain an animal</u>. To have someone **on a short leash** suggests you are controlling their natural exuberance and inclinations for your own benefit, like a pet dog. In other words, they – like your canine companion – are not to be trusted out except on a lead. This figure of speech has been in use since at least the mid 16th century.

But here's the odd thing: the same word could not only denote restraint, but also free rein. <u>Leash</u> originally came from the Latin <u>laxare</u>, meaning to <u>let go</u>, and developed via Old French <u>laisser</u>, meaning to <u>let a dog run on a slack lead</u>. In the 15th century the related word <u>lease</u> could also convey, among other things, a <u>quantity of thread</u>, or the <u>crossing of the warp-threads</u> in the loom.

LINE ☞ CORD, LINEN, ROPE, STRING, THREAD, TOW and YARN

From at least Roman times, the long fibres of flax were called <u>line</u> and they were used to make the thread for <u>linen</u> cloth. All our words incorporating 'line' were originally derived from this idea of a thread. They have come down to us both directly from the Latin <u>linum</u>, meaning a <u>thread of flax</u>, and via Old French <u>ligne</u> in the 14th century; the two words came together in English as <u>line</u>. Lots of similar European words for cords and string were also derived from roots concerning thread.

In language, as in all utilitarian things, form follows function, and there is an obvious progression of meaning here. Our distant ancestors would have used a taut thread to measure any solid object, such as a piece of wood, stone or bone. String, held tight, also provided a **guideline** to ensure that edges were marked and cut perfectly straight. Such measuring aids were used in the earliest forms of geometry and architecture, when ancient early peoples discovered the principles of arcs, circles and scaling things up or down by means of string and pegs. It is impossible to overestimate the importance of this use of thread or cord in the development of human ingenuity and new technologies.

Every time you **draw a line**, talk on a **telephone line**, use a **plumbline**, **hang your washing on the line**, catch fish with a **rod and line**, do a **line drawing**, join a **line-up**, fill in an **outline**, travel by train on **railway lines**, put **a lining** in a drawer or garment, go **line-dancing**, or even when you go **on line** or **off line** using telecoms, you are paying tribute to the wonderful value and usefulness of thread.

As if that weren't enough, there are all sorts of sayings with <u>line</u> in them as figures of speech – making them a double metaphor.

Your fate is supposed to be reflected in the creases in your palms, which have the **life**, **head** and **heart lines** on them, a reference to the **lifeline** – the thread of life spun by the Fates. Consequently your **lifeline** can also mean <u>your appointed lot in life</u>, that which is right and proper for you to do.

To throw someone a lifeline refers to saving a drowning person, but has also come to mean giving someone a way out of a crisis situation. **A line judge** in tennis watches the game to see whether the ball falls inside or outside the white line marked on the ground.

In the early 16th century you might have spoken of **lining your pockets** if you were taking money, often with the suggestion of something illegal, a bribe or theft. If you are **lining your stomach** you are simply having a good meal.

We warn people **not to cross the line** or **get out of line** if they threaten to behave badly. You might say **you should come into line** or **bring him into line** to recall them to their duty or encourage them to give in to peer pressure.

If someone is **mainlining**, I am afraid they are not behaving properly, but are injecting hard drugs into their veins. However, **mainline** is also used to denote the most important railway stations.

Flatlined means dead, because the trace your heart makes on the electro-cardiogram becomes flat. But working to a **deadline** simply means that you must complete some task by a certain date or time, not that you are dead – unless you have a particularly vicious boss. It probably comes from the newspaper trade where, if a writer failed to submit a story on time, it lost its news value and was therefore 'dead'. Another, more sinister, meaning of **deadline** refers to a line drawn round a military prison beyond which an escaping prisoner may be shot dead.

Staying with the Fourth Estate, a **headline** is the main heading for a story in the newspaper, while a **byline** is the writer's name below the heading – a credit that shows he or she wrote the story. A **cutline** is a newspaper caption, the picture over it being known as a <u>cut</u>, from the days before photography, when illustrations were made by wood engravers, and later by steel engravers.

If you say you can **read between the lines**, it means you understand the things that are not being said, but only hinted at, in speech or writing.

To drop someone a line is to write them a letter, and derives from the 18th century custom of letting a note drop informally into the letter-box of the recipient's door. Nowadays, it's more likely to refer to an email or a cell phone text.

Drawing a line under it means recognising that something is finished, ending it and moving on, as if ruling a line under your words when writing. However, **drawing a fine line** is discriminating carefully, usually between two or more abstractions. You might say, '**She drew a fine line between** honesty and politeness' when you asked her what she thought of your new hair style.

Drawing a line in the sand suggests a vain endeavour, since the sea will come and wash it away. But it is also used — especially in bad western movies — to invite confrontation between two characters. It signals, 'That's as far as you go. Step over that at your own risk, pardner.'

All down the line means throughout, while *all along the line*, suggests something that happens repeatedly or continually, and *the end of the line* is the metaphorical terminus of the journey.

Lines have a lot to do with relationships. The phrase *marriage lines* refers to the wedding certificate with its lines of writing. Many people in earlier times would not have been able to read them, making their mark instead of a signature.

Your *lineage* is the line drawn from your ancestors to you — your *lineal* descent from your forebears. Another metaphorical line is used in a team or corporation, to show how you are accountable to your *line manager*, the person above you in the hierarchy. *Lineaments* is an old-fashioned word for a person's facial features and comes from the action of making a line, as in drawing.

In my line of country does not suggest real territory, but an area of knowledge in which you are expert, or at least well informed.

A row or rank of troops can also be called a *line*, and *the thin red line* was a heroic phrase coined by a journalist in the Crimean War. It was said of a small remnant of British troops in their red uniforms *holding the line* against the Russian advance, and has come to mean any group dealing in a similar way with an overwhelming problem, sometimes in a mock-heroic context.

The phrases *thin blue line* and *the grey line* were used during the American Civil War, from the Union blue and Confederate grey uniforms. The Thin Red Line has an American equivalent in *the long grey line*, which refers to the graduates of West Point Military Academy in Virginia, USA. They are said to have a very strong *esprit de corps*, and a sense that past generations of West Pointers are gazing down on them.

We say *hard lines* to commiserate with someone about their lot in life. It was possibly nautical in origin, from the hard taut ropes of the rigging. On the other hand, its opposite meaning, of a happy and fortunate existence, 'the lines have fallen for me in pleasant places,' is a direct quotation from verse six of the 16th Psalm, and carries on with 'yea, I have a goodly heritage'.

A **line** of ships, like the **Cunard Line** or **White Star Line**, provided a regular succession of vessels **plying** the seas between designated ports, as though 'joining up the dots' in a series of thread-like but invisible routes. Hence also **ocean liners** and **ships of the line**.

You might follow **the party line**, meaning sticking to what the policy makers in a certain political party tell you. You will be **in line with** what the leadership wants. Then again, you might **take a strong line** over what you believe, even **laying it on the line**, meaning being insistent about what others should do.

If you are something of a bossyboots, you could insist that others should **toe the line**, a sporting phrase derived from the line behind which competitors stand before the start of a foot race. Apparently, it was first used in print in the metaphoric sense in an 1895 edition of the *Westminster Gazette*.

Your opponents, when disagreeing with you, might take an equally **strong line**, and say you've got hold of the wrong end of the stick, or **got your lines crossed**, meaning that you have misunderstood matters. They might even suggest that you are **shooting a line**, and therefore not being strictly truthful. In reply, you might then complain that you couldn't **get a line on** the whole project, and a sympathetic onlooker would regret that you seemed to be **in the firing line**, implying that your critics were shooting at you, though not, we hope, literally. You might try to get a **hot line** to a friend for advice, which suggests you can make fast, direct contact with them, as if down a telephone line that is hot with urgency.

The idea of **writing out lines** of nonsense as a punishment goes back to the mid 16th century, but the **lines** referring to the script an actor learns only entered our language in the 1880s.

When we say **every cloud has a silver lining** we are using a metaphor that suggests something good can be found even in a grey and gloomy situation. The poet John Milton seems to have popularised the idea of a silver lining to a cloud as a symbol of hope, when he made a character in his masque *Comus* say

Was I deceived, or did a sable cloud
Turn forth her silver lining on the night?

This imagery became popular, and indeed it is now a cliché, as in these doggerel lines of verse written by Ellen Thorneycroft Fowler.

> Though outwardly a gloomy shroud,
> The inner half of every cloud
> Is bright and shining;
> I therefore turn my clouds about,
> And always wear them inside out,
> To show the lining.

And what about the American song *The Wichita Lineman* by Jimmy Webb, first recorded by Glen Campbell, in which a telephone line repair man, high above the ground in his lonely job, tells his love how much he misses her? The refrain reminds her repeatedly that he is still on the line, as in someone on the other end of a phone call. It also carries an unspoken hint of the other meaning of **on the line**; hooked like a helpless fish. Perhaps this admission of vulnerability is what gives the song its haunting resonance.

LINEN ☞ FLAX and LINE

Linen would have been a good bet as a generic term for fabric, even though it is now only used for flax cloth, since it gave rise to lots of **line** words. It comes to us from Latin, where <u>linum</u> meant simply a <u>thread of flax</u>, and <u>lin</u> was <u>linen cloth</u>. From this we get not only the word <u>linen</u>, but also **linseed oil**, the oil pressed from the flax seed, as well as **linoleum** for the floor, which was a <u>floor covering</u>, patented in 1860, made from canvas and an oxidised form of the oil.

We also derived <u>lint</u>, which came by compression of the Middle English word for <u>linen</u> as <u>linnet</u>, or the French <u>linette</u>, from which we also derive **linnet**, a <u>seed-eating bird</u>. Originally <u>lint</u> was used for burning in a tinderbox, as it was flax thread, fluffed up in preparation for spinning, and was very combustible. Flax fluff could also be scraped off linen cloth, as a soft dressing for wounds, still known and used as <u>lint</u>. Also in the late 19th century English adopted the French word <u>lingerie</u>, which meant <u>linen garments</u>, for all types of underwear.

Through French, we also got <u>crinoline</u>, a word coined in 1830 from combining <u>crinus</u>, meaning hair, and <u>linum</u>, <u>linen thread</u>. This stuff was at first a <u>stiff fabric</u>, then a <u>petticoat stuffed with horsehair</u> (like a sofa), and finally a <u>hooped petticoat</u> whose whalebone ribs held out the voluminous skirts of the mid 19th century. <u>Crinoline</u> had the alternative but similar meaning of <u>netting</u>, in particular the <u>netting fitted round warships</u> as a defence against torpedoes. Perhaps the warships bustling along the channel in their defensive skirts were almost as terrifying as Victorian matrons in their bustles and hoops.

We use the phrase **don't wash your dirty linen in public** to warn against talking openly about family scandals or anyone's unsavoury past.

There is a Norse story to account for the discovery of linen, in which a starving shepherd found a cave at the top of a mountain. Inside were three beautiful women. Both they and the walls blazed with jewels, and the poor man realised he was gazing at the goddess Frigga and her handmaidens. The goddess offered him his choice of the jewels, but he asked only for the bunch of blue flowers she held in her hand. At once he found himself outside again, grasping the blossoms. His wife was very scornful at first, but he planted the seeds from the flowers and harvested them. When the harvest came, Frigga visited the couple and showed them how to ret the plants – a process in making thread – and how to spin and weave. The cloth they made was better than anything known so far, and made the couple rich. The blue flower was, of course, the flax plant, *Linum ussitatissimum*.

Before hemp was known, linen ropes would have been more than strong enough for most purposes. There is a story that Xerxes, King of Persia, made his slaves weave linen ropes, from which his engineers devised easily made rope bridges. This innovation took the Greeks by surprise, allowing Xerxes to move his army across the Hellespont into the enemy territory before they were aware of an invasion.

So, we now know where we get the word <u>linen</u> for a <u>textile made of flax</u>, but why is the word for the fabric so different from the common name of the flower from which it comes? True, the Latin botanical name of the plant, *Linum ussitatissimum*, suggests linen. As for flax, the Romans adopted a word from the Greeks, <u>flechten</u> that meant to <u>plait</u>. The linguistic shift between 'p' and 'f' transmuted it into <u>plectere</u> in Latin, and eventually back into English, by a slightly tortuous route, to give us the noun <u>flax</u>.

It seems very likely that the word <u>flax</u> was retained by the poor old peasants, who did the hard and dirty work of treading the flax stems in water, and then leaving them, to <u>rot out</u> (or <u>ret</u>) the fibres from the stems, as part of the preparation. The more refined, specialist weavers who made the cloth from the fine thread used the word <u>linen</u>.

··· *Made From the Same Piece of Cloth* *···*

LINSEY-WOOLSEY

To say something is **all linsey-woolsey** means it is all mixed up — neither one thing nor the other. In speech, it implies that someone is talking nonsense or speaking in a garbled way.

In the 15th century, linsey-woolsey was a mixed fabric made of flax and wool; later it became a dress fabric of inferior, coarse wool weft made on a cotton warp. I have only heard the phrase occasionally in recent years, but both the fabric and its use as a figure of speech were still around when I was young and excitable. '**Slow down**,' I was sometimes told, '**You're talking absolute linsey-woolsey!**'

LOOM ☞ WEAVE

If all you inherited in your Aunt Aggie's will was a loom for weaving on, you might be a bit disappointed, but it really would be an **heirloom**. A <u>loom</u> could mean originally any <u>utensil</u> or <u>implement</u>. The term eventually linked with the <u>heir</u> to an estate, and became a <u>chattel that can be left to someone in a will</u>.

One useful implement was the frame on which threads could be made to cross each other under tension, for weaving cloth, and gradually, this **loom** took over the word. Like many other <u>tool</u> words, **loom** is used as slang for a penis.

Saying that someone **looms over you** comes from a different source, a Dutch dialect word for things that are slack, soft or misty, and has to do with <u>moving slowly</u>. Seamen in past times used it for the way rocks or ships appear in exaggerated form when one is sailing near to shore in foggy weather.

MADE UP OUT OF WHOLE CLOTH ☞ CLOTH

To make something up out of whole cloth means to tell a story that is completely untrue from beginning to end. Cloth would originally be sold as it came from the loom, in a set width, but once it was cut, manufacturers and sellers might cheat the purchaser by not giving full measure. In the same way, you could not be sure of the truth of a story **cut from whole cloth**, which became a common saying from the 15th century.

People who have much in common are said to be **cut from the same cloth**, or **out of the same piece of cloth**, as if they came from a single large piece of fabric.

I should perhaps have dedicated this book to **St Amphibalus**, as he was **made up out of whole cloth**. In the 8th century the Venerable Bede is said to have originally misread <u>amphibalus</u>, a word for <u>cloak</u>, as the name of a person. Geoffrey of Monmouth and subsequent writers repeated the error. The story ran and ran. Medieval monks created a whole history of St Amphibalus: how he was born in Wales, how he was one of the companions of St Alban, and how he was eventually murdered along with 1,000 other martyrs.

I have developed a great fondness for my little woolly saint. As the prefix <u>amphi-</u> comes from the Greek and means something like <u>double</u> or <u>of both sides</u>, I have come to see **St Amphibalus** not as a traditional woollen cloak but as a <u>smart, double-breasted suit</u>, an imaginary saint better <u>suited</u> to our times.

MATERIAL ☞ CLOTH, FABRIC and STUFF

Madonna calls herself a Material Girl in one of her songs. I don't think she means she's like a cloth doll. Why do we use the word <u>material</u> as yet another synonym for <u>cloth</u>? Once again, an apparently textile term proves to have a different source. The Romans used the word <u>materialis</u> to mean any form of <u>matter</u>, and eventually, the word came into English, thanks to the Normans, via the Old French word <u>materiel</u>. In the 17th century it acquired the meaning of something basic that could be worked upon, or elaborated, such as a document and, of course, many documents were made of cloth or vellum, creating a link to textiles.

MAWKIN ☞ RAG

At your next pub quiz here's a bit of trivia you might spring on your friends. A **mawkin** is a dialect word for a scarecrow and also has the very specific meaning of a <u>rag used to clean out a baker's oven</u>. It came originally from <u>Malkin</u>, a diminutive form of the name <u>Maud</u> or <u>Mathilda</u>, which descended into a <u>female imp</u>, a <u>slut</u> and so to a <u>mop</u> or <u>bundle of rags</u>. It may also have given us <u>mawkingly</u> meaning slovenly, now obsolete, and possibly **mawkish**, to suggest something sickly, full of false sentiment, lacking strength and robustness.

MERINO PURE ☞ FLEECE and WOOL

Would you be pleased to be described as a **Merino Pure**? You should be. The wool from Merino sheep is prized for its softness and strength, and is still regarded as making the finest cloth. Merinos were imported into Australia from Europe at the end of the 18th century and, in the 19th century, the members of the very first colonising families — especially in New South Wales — were praised as **Merinos Pure**.

MISS MUFFETT ☞ SPIDER

Little Miss Muffett
Sat on a tuffet,
Eating her curds and whey.
There came a great spider
And sat down beside her,
And frightened Miss Muffett away.

Who was this young woman with a severe spider phobia, was she a real person, and can we find out her first name? Well, some authorities think the rhyme was a skit on the work of an entomologist, Dr Thomas Muffett, who died in 1604. He wrote a treatise on *The Silkworm and all her Flies*, which became popular posthumously. He had a daughter to whom the rhyme was supposed to refer – and we know that her first name was, appropriately enough, **Patience**. I have been unable to trace the family of the importunate spider, so she must remain anonymous.

MITOSIS

Here's one for you scholars. **Mitosis** is the biological term for one type of cell division (the other, if you want to know, is meiosis). Under a microscope, you can see that the nucleus breaks into an appearance like a mass of fine threads, and so they named the process with the Greek word for thread. In earlier times, Latin and Greek were the languages in which scientists all over the world could communicate freely with each other, so most scientific names reflect this. Mind you, I think scientists are also a bit inclined to show off, using such terms instead of just saying, 'Oh, they look a bit like thread', as the rest of us would.

NEEDLE ☞ PIN and SEW

Scissors and string, scissors and string,
When a man's single he lives like a king,
Needles and pins, needles and pins,
When a man marries, his trouble begins.

Well, all I can do is point out that statistics show married men live longer than bachelors, but married women have a shorter life expectancy than spinsters. I make no other comment.

Pins and needles are as vital a part of the textile worker's armoury as a sword is to a hero. They started out as thorns and fish bones, or slivers of animal bone or horn, then thin wires of copper, bronze, and iron, and finally of steel.

The earliest reference to a <u>needle</u> in English literature may well be in Langland's Piers the Plowman. It is called a <u>paknedel</u>, which would be very large and strong for sewing up goods in sackcloth, the essential packaging for anything that needed storing or transporting.

One base word for sewing was <u>siw</u>, from which we get **sew**. A second root was the Indo-European word <u>ne</u>. This became <u>nethlo</u>, from which comes our **needle**, and also **nerve** and **neural**.

An ordinary household in past times would possess only a few needles for their own use, or to be lent out to trustworthy friends by the lady of the house. They would be returned to the **needle-case** attached to her belt to be kept under her watchful eye. A needle had to be crafted by skilled artisans, and its cost was considerable. The plot of a 16th century comedy, *Gammer Gurton's Needle*, revolves entirely round the misplacing of this vital item.

Needles have been made in Europe since the 14th century, and the industry probably came to England from Spain, where the Moors had already been making them for a long time. In London, the medieval craft guilds preserved their rights jealously, so needle making was a restricted industry. This led eventually to the relocation of the manufacture of needles to designated places such as Redditch in Worcestershire. The practice of stitching has been known as <u>needlework</u> since the early 17th century, hence <u>needlewoman</u> and <u>needleworker</u>.

The arms of the Worshipful Company of Needlemakers shows <u>three needles</u>, crowned, on a shield. The supporters are Adam and Eve, and she is holding a needle. These arms gave the name **Threadneedle Street**, corrupted from <u>three needles</u>, to a street in the original square mile of the City of London. The present Bank of England is on the site of the old Needlemakers Hall; hence the Bank's ironic nickname, **The Old Lady of Threadneedle Street**, first bestowed in a cartoon by James Gilray, the 18th century caricaturist and political satirist.

To needle somebody is to annoy them deliberately, similar to the phrase **to nettle them**. In 19th-century tailor's slang, <u>to cop the needle</u> or <u>to take the needle</u> meant to become annoyed, due to the irritation of running a needle into your finger. Not surprisingly, there were many more colloquial sayings about needles in the past, when hand sewing was common. Many have vanished from our speech. Rhyming slang gave us <u>needle and pin</u> for <u>gin</u>, and <u>needle and thread</u> for <u>bread</u>. A <u>needlewoman</u> was a prostitute, whose <u>needle-case</u> was her vagina, and so a <u>needle</u> meant a penis. But it could also be a card sharp or a thief. A <u>needle-jerker</u> was a contemptuous name for a tailor.

Even in the 18th century, not all women accepted that they, or their occupations, were inferior to those of men. The contemporary poet, Esther Lewis said

> Are simple women only fit
> To dress, to darn, to flower or knit,
> To mind the distaff or the spit?
> Why are the needle and the pen
> Thought incompatible by men?

The phrase *a needle in a haystack* for something almost impossible to find gives us a striking picture of someone dropping her needle while sitting on a bale of hay, but it was far more likely to be a 'hay needle' that was lost. This two-foot-long metal spike (that's about 60 cm for the metrically-minded), with a point at one end and a ring at the other, was used to push the hay into square bales and keep them in place. Such an implement could easily be left in and lost, but doesn't create quite as colourful an image.

When Jesus said, 'It is easier for a camel to go through the eye of a needle, than for a rich man to enter into the Kingdom of Heaven,' he was using a picturesque exaggeration to make his point. *A camel going through the eye of a needle* has become a saying for doing something impossible. It has been suggested that Jesus referred to a particular gateway in ancient Jerusalem, called the Needle's Eye because it was so narrow that camels could barely squeeze through. Or perhaps that is just the rationalisation of a rich man hoping to improve his chances of salvation by starving his camels.

Another and stranger feature known as **The Needle's Eye** is a pyramidal tower in South Yorkshire, UK, that is pierced by a carriageway. The legend says that the Marquis of Rockingham created it in order to fulfil a bet that he could drive his coach and horses through the eye of a needle.

A famous outcrop of soft chalk on the west coast of the Isle of Wight, UK, has worn into a series of pinnacles that stick dramatically out of the sea and are known as **The Needles**.

Pins and needles describes the feeling of tingling nerves in the body when you have let a limb 'go to sleep' by cutting off the blood supply while sitting in an awkward posture.

Oh, and be sure to close your mouth and your nose anywhere near a dragonfly. It is known colloquially in some places as a ***darning needle*** and might sew up your orifices, or go straight into one ear and out at the other – so best cover them, too. You'll need three hands to do all that.

My friend's mother had a little saying for when she was annoyed with her daughter, whom she regarded as being overly generous. She always lowered her voice to almost whisper it, so that my friend also, and quite unconsciously did the same when telling me, 'You're too generous for your own good; you'd give your arse away and shit through the eye of a needle!'

NET ☞ KNIT, KNOT and WEB

We have already looked at how knots by themselves are useful enough, but when you start putting a lot of them together by knotting, twisting, tying and plaiting, you can make a larger, continuous piece of work with a wonderful variety of purposes.

Netting is the process of making an openwork fabric by knotting cords at intervals, and was probably one of the earliest form of weaving. The loom-weaving of textiles was a relatively complicated technique and came quite late in human development, although still before our ancestors settled down as farming communities.

No one quite knows where the word net comes from, though the Old English mesh may have come from the Latin nassa, which was a wicker basket for catching fish. There are related words in Dutch, Danish, Swedish and German, all coming from an old Germanic root, netz. It may also have links with other words for knotting, and twisting, from the Latin nodus, a knot, from which we get **node**.

Many different cultures have come up with the net, not only for its use as a real object, but also as a symbol of how the world and its people interlink and mesh with one another in mutual interdependence.

A net's pattern of crossing lines held great significance in prehistoric times, symbolising the waters of life and female fertility, as shown by the patterns on innumerable artefacts linked with thread processes, including spindle whorls and loom weights.

There is a story of the Norse god Loki, the mischief maker, in one of the frequent times when he had made himself so unpopular he had to run away and hide. He invented the first net, so as to catch fish to eat. When he saw Thor, the god of thunder, coming, he spitefully burned it on his fire before escaping. The god was able to reconstruct the net from the pattern in the ashes, and gave it to mankind.

The origin of netting a profit, meaning making a clear profit, sounds as if it should come from fishing for money. But in reality, the term has links with the French net or nette (in the feminine form) that also gave us net as neat, meaning clean and tidy, and has no textile connection. The accidental association with fishing may be what keeps the figure of speech in the language.

Netting is also a dialect word for the use of urine in the dyeing industry. Stale urine acts as a mordant to fix the colour of the dye. More importantly, it assists in the production of alum for the same purpose. It is said that the term taking the piss originates in the collection of urine in the 16th century, when it was brought by ship from London and Newcastle to the alum industry near Whitby, North Yorkshire, UK.

Even earlier, in ancient Rome, large earthenware jars were left at every major junction for male passers-by to use as urinals. The urine was collected every night and used in laundries to whiten cloth, and it was a civic duty to contribute. Imagine a Roman citizen telling his wife, 'It's essential I drink these 30 amphorae of beer, so that I can do my duty to the laundry.' She really would think he was taking the piss.

Weavers also collected urine, and there was a superstition that it worked best if it came from a red-headed woman. That sounds wacky, but perhaps it is true, as redheads possess more of a chemical called pheomelanin in their urine, a substance linked with melanin, the pigment that gives colour to our skin and hair.

ODDS AND ENDS ☞ CABBAGE

The word remnant came from a French word, remenant, meaning that which remains when part is taken away. The later English equivalent for the end of a roll of fabric was an odd end. In fabric shops today, remnants is the term used for pieces of left-over textiles, and the phrase *odds and ends* has come to refer to any miscellaneous collection of objects.

PATCH ☞ CROSSPATCH, PIECING and QUILT

The word <u>patch</u> was probably a variation of <u>piece</u> and originally came from a lost word in the ancient Celtic language of Gaul. It is thought that this word would have had the base <u>pett</u>, and it became <u>petia</u> in Latin. It probably became <u>peche</u> or <u>pieche</u>, in Old French, a dialect variation linking the word to <u>piece</u>. From there, it crossed over to England as the Anglo-Norman <u>pece</u>, to give us both <u>piece</u> and <u>patch</u>, often used interchangeably, and even yielded **peat** to burn on the fire.

By the 15th century, <u>patch</u> tended to mean making a clumsy repair to clothes or shoes. The term <u>botched</u> was also used for applying a patch clumsily, and we still describe a <u>botched</u> or <u>bodged</u> job as one hastily and badly done. It is of unknown origin, though possibly derived from <u>boss</u>, a lump. A <u>botch</u> or <u>blotch</u> was also a <u>boil</u>, <u>ulcer</u> or <u>pimple</u>, and a <u>bodger</u> was a dialect word for a rustic carpenter who made greenwood chairs. Because of the implication of a hasty or inadequate mend, **patching things up**, such as a quarrel or a friendship, suggests an improvement that's unlikely to last; the phrase has been used in this way since the later 19th century.

From the early 16th century on, we have used **patch** figuratively to mean a small area of something, while **to strike a bad** or **difficult patch** denotes a period of trouble or bad luck. In police work, the bobby on the beat would describe his local neighbourhood as his **patch** – the bit for which he was responsible. If we were comparing our work, I might say **yours is not a patch on mine**, meaning you're simply nowhere near as good as me.

<u>Patchwork</u> involves sewing many small pieces of cloth together to produce a larger fabric. Cloth has always been prized and ever since sewing began it has been important to save fabric and mend garments. Putting a patch on a garment extends its useful life, and joining scraps together creates an economical and colourful fabric. Today this technique has grown to be a pleasure and an art form in its own right.

Poetic writers sometimes describe the countryside as being **a patchwork of fields**, having the beauty and colour variation of a quilt laid over the earth. Or it can be a figure of speech to suggest a medley of incongruous and jumbled things, something **patchy**. We might also speak of **a patchwork of lies**. It's a pity that **patchery**, once commonly used for the process of putting things together, is no longer in use.

Those who do the so-called English form of patchwork know that it is done using paper templates around which the fabric pieces are tacked until they can be sewn together, edge to edge. Patchwork pieces require a lot of paper, which was expensive and in short supply in past centuries, and needlewomen therefore cut up anything suitable that came to hand, such as old letters. Apparently John Evelyn's famous diary very nearly suffered this fate, but was rescued at the last minute. We craftswomen sometimes complain that our traditional skills are not valued as they should be, but it is chastening to think that we have also been guilty in the past of destroying so much fascinating historical material in order to support our hobbies.

PIECING ☞ CROSSPATCH, PATCH and QUILT

We speak of *piecing together* a story or puzzle. That may seem an obvious metaphor derived from sewing cloth; in fact, it's a little more complex. Piece goods were pieces of fabric of a set length, sold for a particular purpose. The Latin word pettia gave us the original piece, described as any separate portion or fragment in medieval times. However, by the 16th century the word had developed a number of more specific meanings relating to portions, including one for a length of cloth.

It's rather a shame that industrialisation did away with jobs such as that of a piecener, an apprentice in a spinning mill who filled the frames with rovings, pieced up the threads and joined the cardings and slivers for the slubber. I've only a vague idea of what he was actually doing, but it reads a bit like a poem.

PIN ☞ NEEDLE

Pins were always important, were needed for many more purposes than needles and were quite expensive. Those wealthy enough would use them to hold their clothing together, while poor folk had to make do with strings or linen ties. The Celts, following Roman fashions, employed brooches and decorative items for the same purpose, and in the USA brooches are still known as pins.

The word pin came from the Latin pinna, which meant a wing, fin, feather, or any pointed thing. From this root we also get pinion and pinnacle. Thanks to the stylish French, we refer to *panache*, which originally meant a plume of feathers, often worn in the hat, and so its modern use to describe a dashing attitude or smart presentation.

We seem to have a great many figures of speech derived from pins. **To pin someone down** is to hold them strictly to a promise, or get them to be totally specific in what they say with **pinpoint accuracy**. This phrase always symbolised something focused, but entered common parlance in the Second World War to describe precision strikes by bomber crews. **To pinpoint something** is a more general term to suggest identifying an objective exactly.

Not to put too fine a point on it is used to give emphasis to a statement, by being direct rather than going on and on – **going straight to the point**, in fact.

You might say **don't pin it on me** to repudiate blame, as if someone were going to pin a notice of fault on your back. But it also harks back to feudal times, when a serf could be compelled to wear the badge of his overlord and follow him in battle, whether he wished to or not. A **pinafore** is – literally – a protective piece of cloth that you pinned <u>afore</u>, or <u>in front</u> of you.

In merry pin or **in good pin** has now gone out of use, but both meant happy and healthy, or in fine fettle, and may be linked to the <u>pin</u> or <u>peg</u> used for tuning a stringed instrument.

We say **sharp as a pin** or **bright as a new pin**, meaning clever, and **neat as a new pin** or **clean as a new pin** to mean a very tidy room or person. In the days before mass production, fashioning pins and needles was extremely complicated and involved many different steps, including arduous polishing. It has been calculated that in the 18th century it took more than 20 people to make a pin.

Pins are slang for legs, as in **get on your pins**, telling you to get up, or describing you as **shaky on your pins** if you are a bit wobbly. Describing someone as **being on pins and needles**, meaning impatient or nervous, suggests that they are poised uncomfortably on the sharp points of pins – or just that they are hopping about impatiently on their own **pins**.

A **pinhead**, however, is a fool. If I call you that or say **I don't give a pin for your views**, or that something you say is **not worth a pin**, it means that I consider you or your ideas to be almost worthless. You might rise above my insults by saying **they're only a pinprick**, meaning a small annoyance, so minor as to be unworthy of further comment.

It is not that long since women in the Western world were unable to keep their own property on marriage, and **pin money** was traditionally the small sum of money a wife could keep for herself. The origin of the term is not entirely clear, though it may date from the 15th century, when pins were so expensive as to feature in wills. Pins were sometimes given 'for your wife' instead of small change. As pins became cheaper, the term came to mean a very small amount, received in addition to regular income or trifling sums of cash, considered suitable for a woman's needs.

Pins were sometimes used instead of small sums of money in the USA as well. In *Penrod*, Booth Tarkington's classic comic novel of 1914, the children set up a museum. Entry was by pin, with the going rate apparently being 1 cent for 20 pins.

The value of pins is proverbial. ***It is a sin to steal a pin*** is appropriately short and to the point, while ***he that will not stoop for a pin will never be worth a pound*** could be said to be economically truthful.

Pins were also noted in folklore for their healing properties, probably because metals were considered magic. The Celts made votive offerings of weapons and other metal objects into sacred lakes, and we still throw pins or coins into Holy wells for luck.

Pins feature in dozens of superstitions; here are just a few. You could protect yourself against witches and fairies, who were said to fear cold iron, by putting pins into a bottle or sticking them in a door lintel to protect the house. Witches themselves were said to stick pins into effigies of those they wished to harm, a practice still found in voodoo ceremonies.

All pins used in making a shroud should be buried with it, but all pins must be removed from a wedding dress or they will bring bad luck – particularly to anyone hugging the bride. You might put a pin through a candle to make a wish, or it could add an element of chance to an auction, the winning bid being the one spoken as the pin dropped out with the melted wax.

And, of course, most people can still quote

> *See a pin and pick it up,*
> *All the day you'll have good luck.*
> *See a pin and let it lay,*
> *And you'll rue it all the day.*

The traditional fairy tale *Little Red Riding Hood* was originally a story from 17th century France, and probably dealt with the initiation of a young girl into the local sewing sisterhood, as this commercial activity was carried out by families in their own homes. She has to choose between the path of needles and the path of pins.

She chooses needles, perhaps signifying acceptance of her vocation, but they are longer than pins and allow the wolf to reach Grandmother's house first.

Samuel Pepys, who recorded many of his amatory adventures in his diaries, recounts ingenuously how he stood by a 'pretty, modest maid' at St Dunstan's Church on August 18th, 1666. He tried to take her hand during the sermon, and she fended him off with a pin. Those of us who have suffered similar unwelcome advances on the Tube (the London Underground) in rush hour could hold anniversary parties in August on the Circle Line, in celebration of the spirited maid, except that if we took out pins we'd be arrested for carrying offensive weapons.

Up until the early 20th century, women used long hat pins, taken from their elaborate Edwardian hats, for similar protective purposes, but this went out with shingled hair and greater sexual freedom.

Originally a **pin-up girl** was a picture of a girlfriend, sweetheart, wife or a scantily clad film star, pinned up on the lockers of servicemen far from home during the Second World War. Now it is shortened to **pin-up**, for any glamorous picture of a young woman.

How many angels can dance on the point of a pin? This impossible philosophical question was much debated as an exercise in logic in the Middle Ages, though it was wholly illogical, since a spiritual being such as an angel has no weight or mass, and the point of a pin is an infinitely small area. In the era BT, or Before Television, people pursued important topics like these, while we have to make do with quiz shows and home design makeovers to get our intellectual stimulus.

We exclaim about a sudden or profound silence that **you could have heard a pin drop**, which probably goes back to the early 19th century writer, Leigh Hunt, who said (in *The Story of Rimini*), 'A pin-drop silence strikes o'er all the place.'

PLAIT ☞ KNOT, PLIGHT, PLY and WEAVE

Plaiting is the action used to make braids, and is another simple form of weaving. Like **ply**, plait came from the Latin plictum or plicitum for a fold. As with the shuttle, the origin of braid lies in the movement rather than the end result. A braid came from the Old English bregthan, which meant to make jerky movements from side to side. Perhaps this is where **to upbraid** someone comes from, it certainly could give a vivid picture of slapping someone on both cheeks or pulling them by the hair. The word **bridle** has the same origin in plaiting a braid, an article that could then be used to control a horse.

The Old French pleit, also from the Latin, plicare, was a fold or a manner of folding, which became superseded in English by pleat. By the mid 15th century, it meant to gather loose or flowing cloth into regular, fixed folds, but was also used figuratively for anything that appeared folded.

PLIGHT ☞ PLAIT and PLY

The Latin plicitum or plictum, meaning a fold, gave us pleat and plait for a particular folding or twisting thread together. It also gives us the word *plight*, which carries the sense of being in a particular state or condition. From it we also get the old-fashioned *plighting your troth*, for pledging your loyalty or good faith to your marriage partner. A *plight* also refers to a predicament or dangerous situation you might be in – though hopefully, the last two situations don't resemble each other.

PLUSH ☞ VELVET

Some of us would like a *plush lifestyle*. In times past, those who lived – and dressed – in high style sought to surround themselves with a rare and costly type of velvet, possessing a very long nap. The French, who called it peluche, later anglicised as plush, developed this fabric in the 16th century. Soon it was used as a general term of approbation, and anything very luxurious could be referred to as *plush*. Sadly, this fabric didn't wear very well, but the nobility dressed both their clowns and their footmen in it, so the poor (who made do with plain but sturdy stuff) referred to it as fool's cloth.

PLY ☞ PLAIT and PLIGHT

Even fragile fibres such as grass, straw, and stringy plants become strong and versatile when twisted into a bundle. However, it is probably obvious to the perceptive reader, or anyone who has tried to twist up two threads, that there is one disadvantage to this process. As soon as you let go of the end, the thread untwists again.

How do you solve this problem? Simple. You take a second thread, turn it so that the twist goes in the opposite direction, one with an 's' twist, the other with a 'z', and twine the two together. This is called *plying* and makes the thread much stronger.

The word *ply* comes down to us from the Latin plicare, a verb meaning to fold. The noun, plictum or plicitum, gave us pleat, plait and plight, all therefore related. The word then evolved along several different paths.

From this Latin source the French took their word emplier, meaning to enfold, to enwrap, to entangle, to involve, both for thread and for fabric. This came back into English as the second syllable of words such as **apply**, **supply**, **employ**, **imply**, **simple**, and **supple**. The use of the old-fashioned term **a girl plying her needle**, or **plying the oars** to mean rowing, makes use of a shortened form of **apply**, in its sense of working diligently at something. We still say **you must apply yourself** to the task, to urge someone to knuckle down and get to work. And an **application** for a job or a place at university comes from this source.

To ply also means to take sail to windward. It is impossible to sail directly against the wind, so the boat has to turn about and tack from one side to the other, making a little headway each time. Although the ship's wake makes an attractive zigzag pattern, like folds, it is much more likely the phrase came about because tacking is hard work to which you have to **apply** yourself.

Ships also **plied** between ports, and this then came to mean to attend in a particular place repeatedly for trade on land. The dictionary says this meaning took residence on land in the 19th century because cabs and carriages went to and fro between certain spots, like a ship tacking. This habitual pattern eventually extended to anyone walking up and down the street or standing in an accustomed place in the market to buy and sell goods or services, thus **plying their trade**.

We use another figure of speech derived from **ply** when we **display** a flag, as it is a combination of the Latin dis meaning un and plicare, fold. It was used of both flags and sails in Medieval Latin and then came to us by way of the Old French despleier. This notion of spreading out is retained in the English word **splay** as in **he walked with a splay-footed gait**.

From plicare we got not only the English word fold, but also **pliable**, meaning things that can be folded or twisted like fabric and thread. Sometimes **impliable** is used to suggest stiffness or obduracy. People are described as **pliable** if they can be persuaded of something and are flexible in their approach to life, or we might say they were **pliant** or **compliant**, meaning the same thing. Even the use of **pliers**, as a tool for holding metal so that it can be bent, developed from the same word in the 16th century.

A lot of the words that came directly into English in the 14th and 15th centuries from the Latin plicare had already lost their textile meanings. **Complicate** is one, presumably because you are obscuring something simple with many layers, and you might become **perplexed**, another word derived from plait in the 16th century. The folds emerge again in **plywood**, with its layers of wood glued together alternating the direction of the grain to give greater strength. **Implicated** means wrapped up with something or entangled, as in 'Guy Fawkes was **implicated** in the Gunpowder Plot'.

POINTILLISM

The French Impressionists transformed the art world in the late 19th century. One school within Impressionism was **pointillism**: creating an image by innumerable little dots of bright coloured paint, very close together. The eye of the viewer would 'read' the dots as a picture from the right distance, and mix the colours in the brain to make all the shades and tones. So, 'What's that got to do with textiles?' you might ask. The word <u>pointe</u> is French for stitch, and a <u>pointille</u> is the diminutive, so paintings by Georges Seurat and his followers were making <u>little stitches on canvas</u> – truly an inspiration to all embroiderers.

POP GOES THE WEASEL ☞ NEEDLE and WEAVE

Many people have heard the song *Pop Goes the Weasel*, and may know something about its origins in music hall. It gathered a variety of new verses over time.

> *Half a pound of tuppenny rice,*
> *Half a pound of treacle,*
> *Mix it up and make it nice*
> *Pop goes the weasel.*
> *A penny for a spool of thread,*
> *A penny for a needle.*
> *That's the way the money goes,*
> *Pop goes the weasel.*

French silk weavers were Protestant Huguenots, driven out of France in the 17th century by religious persecution. They settled in parts of London, particularly in Soho and Spitalfields. There were music halls in nearby Hoxton, and the popular singers there took old folksongs and gave them an up-to-date twist. These might be sung to several different tunes, for example one was a version of the old rhyme *Here We Go Round the Mulberry Bush* which may refer to silkworm food. Another version became a skit on how the poor spent their money, down at the Eagle pub.

> *Up and down the City Road,*
> *In and out of the Eagle.*
> *That's the way the money goes,*
> *Pop goes the weasel.*

The <u>weasel</u> is variously considered as the popping sound of the spinning machine at the end of its cycle, or rhyming slang for <u>weasel and stoat</u> for <u>coat</u>, or a <u>flat iron</u> used by tailors and known as a <u>weasel</u> which could be <u>popped</u> – that is to say, <u>pawned</u> – in order to bridge a cash flow gap in the family's finances.

QUILT ☞ CROSSPATCH and PATCH

Those who are outsiders to the enchanted world of quilters may become confused over the relationship between patchwork and quilting.

Quilting started as a means of adding warmth and strength to a garment. In cold stone castles and peasants' hovels alike, thick padded garments were essential in winter. In particular, a soldier could reduce chafing and add a little protection from blows, arrows and stab wounds by wearing a padded lining under his armour. The layers of padding needed to be held down at intervals to keep them in place, and the stitching might be plain or could create elaborate patterns. The lines of stitching could be made more decorative on the upper surface, but the layers might be held down with random stitches, knots or even beads. <u>Patchwork</u>, on the other hand, is the joining together of small pieces of fabric. Such work is often, but not necessarily, used as the top layer of a padded quilt, hence the confusion.

The word <u>quilt</u> came from the Latin word <u>culchita</u>, originally meaning a <u>mattress</u>, and the sense that a <u>quilt</u> referred to something padded and stitched down at intervals can be seen from the medieval Latin term <u>culcita puncta</u>, which meant <u>pricked mattress</u>. <u>Culchita</u> is related to the Sanskrit <u>kurcas</u>, a <u>bundle</u>, and came to us from the French <u>cuilte</u>, so it gradually changed from something you <u>lie down on</u> to a <u>warm covering over you</u>.

The verb <u>to quilt</u> wasn't in clear use until the 16th century. At that time it was also used figuratively as in, for example, *to **quilt*** poems or religious writings together as a book.

There was a folk superstition that a girl would die unmarried if she made a quilt on her own, which suggests a high degree of social approval for sewing together. Even so, there was not quite such a strong tradition of holding quilting bees in Britain as there was in the USA. For example, professionals made the majority of 19th century quilts in Wales, and few completely homemade ones have survived. If a household could afford it, a travelling seamstress was employed to provide quilts meant for special occasions. Such a woman would stay in the house for the duration of her task. It was said that one could expect a quilt to be finished in two weeks.

The designs of some of the earlier Welsh quilts, made in woollen flannel, have been analysed and shown to share many common features with those made by the Pennsylvania Amish. This is understandable, given the trade and family links between Wales and the USA, particularly Pennsylvania. Much of the distinctive character of Welsh quilts comes from their traditional hand-stitched patterns and the reverse sides of some quilts show these particularly well. Incidentally, there were so many Welsh settlers at the time that it was a toss up between a Welsh name and an English one for the colony. Quaker William Penn got fed up waiting for the Welsh to decide on a name and declared it would be Penn's Woods – Pennsylvania hence forward.

Anyone making a quilt knows she is using a wonderful means of silent communication. Quilts have been created to commemorate the lives of many gay people who have died of AIDS, to mark historic events and to make political statements or even hide secrets. A patchwork and quilted chasuble dating from the mid 16th century still survives in Cornwall, UK. Priests of the then-banned Roman Catholic religion may have used it, the idea being that if the soldiers came you could hide the garment among the ordinary household quilts.

One of the most inspiring stories in the world of textiles, in which quilts became a language in themselves, was their use in the time of slavery in the plantations of the American South. We are still discovering the meanings hidden in these quilts or 'road maps,' which helped escaping slaves and their sympathisers to communicate secretly with each other. It is only comparatively recently that black Americans have begun to share the stories and codes passed down to them, and there is some uncertainty as to how extensive this practice was.

It was illegal to teach slaves to read and write, but because many came from African cultures possessing a highly sophisticated system of secret societies, they had a tradition of using textile decoration to express a symbolic language. Thus it proved fairly easy to adapt such memory work to provide maps, and also to show sources of food and shelter or warnings of danger by incorporating them in patchwork quilts. Even the style, placing and numbers of the joining stitches could be used to convey vital information. Just like road signs or billboards for the traveller, different quilts could be hung out over fences, as if for airing, without attracting attention. By such means, runaways could find their way to freedom on the so-called 'underground railway,' the network of known tracks and safe houses set up by freed slaves such as Harriet Tubman, and by Abolitionists. These brave people risked life and liberty to oppose a cruel and inhuman trade.

If you are floppy from exhaustion like a villain in the last moments of a movie, the victorious hero might **throw you around like a rag doll**. **Raggedy-Ann** is just such a traditional American doll, originally sewn out of rags. The term **ragtime** for the late 19th-century precursor to American jazz is of uncertain origin, but may be because the syncopation makes for a ragged melody.

Our word rag, meaning a scrap of cloth, comes from Old Norse rogg, denoting a tuft of fur. It then became roggvathr, meaning tufted, and almost certainly gave us ragged from which rag was a back formation in the 13th century. However, there are other uses of the word that are quite separate, such as rag for rough building stone, a form which is very old and of unknown origin. Also venerable is the use of the term to rag someone meaning to taunt them, possibly derived from a Danish word for a grudge.

It would seem, therefore, that to rag someone, or a rag (noisy and disorderly anti-authoritarian behaviour), or to lose your rag (lose your temper) are not textile-derived terms. Nor is Rag Week, a week when almost anything goes for university students, taking part in stunts such as bed racing down the high street in order to collect money for charity.

However, there are plenty of figurative uses of the terms rag and ragged for what the dictionary defines as an insignificant scrap of fabric. A small bit of food, or anything left over or broken could be described as **a rag**, and even your feelings might be **ragged**. When tired, you might be **worn to a rag** because someone has **run you ragged**.

Some terms are more insulting than others. Don't, whatever you do, describe an engineer or the man who does your car as an **oily rag** or, worse, an **oily toe-rag**, unless you want a face-wash with one. This phrase is sometimes used as a general term of abuse, as in **You are a disgusting toe-rag**. The feet, being in contact with the ground, are regarded as dirty and disreputable, and presumably the image it conjures up of a lower extremity, injured and oozing body fluids through a rag of a bandage is meant to describe you as the lowest of the low in a very dramatic way.

Anything ragged in the sense of having frayed edges or being made of rags can be used figuratively. **Ragged Robin** is a common wildflower, *Lychnis flocuculi*, so called because of the tattered-looking petals.

If you are not really poor you might speak of your best clothes ironically as your **glad rags**, a phrase coined in early 19th-century America.

In a similar self-deprecating way, you might say, '**What, this old rag?**' when complimented on your dress. **I haven't a rag to wear**, or **I haven't a rag to my back** is a similar exaggeration. What you mean is, 'In spite of three full wardrobes, five bin bags of clothes and having taken up the whole of the spare bedroom with my Imelda Marcos shoe collection, I never have anything to wear.'

The textile trade, especially that part devoted to women's clothes, is therefore known as the **rag trade**, to acknowledge this female inability to wear anything but 'rags', no matter how much they spend on them.

There are several versions of why someone might **chew the rag**. It could be just an argumentative discussion, from British Army slang of the 19th century, either as a childish pastime or in the sense of bullying. On the other hand, in the early days of the North American settlers it seems they took over the Native American habit of chewing tobacco leaves; sailors on long trips often ran out of supplies and were reduced to chewing anything they could get their teeth into. A **red rag** is also old slang for the tongue, which suggests flapping your tongue in talk. We could stay all day **chewing the rag** without deciding if one, all three, or none of these is the true source of the phrase.

We speak of something known to be highly provocative as **like a red rag to a bull**. Although bulls are probably colour-blind, the Spanish bullfighters flap their red cloaks to make them fight. The idea that red things enrage animals goes back as far as the 16th century, but it is likely to be the flapping action that does this, not the colour.

We probably read a cheap and sensational newspaper from cover-to-cover when we think no one is looking, so why do we call it **a rag** to express our contempt for its contents? Paper made from rags is much more expensive and desirable than that made from wood pulp, and pulp fiction is the equivalent term of contempt given to sensational novels of no literary merit. Answers, please, to be sent on the most beautiful handmade Indian cotton paper.

Rags have always been regarded as significant in folklore and magic. Because they are cloth in its raw state, or degraded clothing, they often have very negative associations. Witches are often said to be dressed in rags, or to use them in black magic. Here is a Scottish spell, used to raise the wind in order to destroy a neighbour's crops or sink ships at sea. If you recited this while beating a wet rag on a stone, it was said the wind would not die down till the rag became dry.

> I knock this rag upon this stane,
> To raise the wind in the devil's name.
> It shall not lie until I please again.

In the early part of the 20th century, there were no disposable pads for menstruation. Women wore diapers or makeshift pads made out of rags that had to be washed every day, so a term for menstruating was **to be on the rag** or **riding the rag**, and menstruation itself might be euphemistically referred to as **the rag**.

We speak of someone who succeeds in life, whether financially or in some other way, as **going from rags to riches**. This scenario is a staple plot for many fairy stories, of which the best known is probably Cinderella. The basic motif is a despised and persecuted girl who is reduced to dressing in rags, sleeping in ashes and doing menial work. Later, she is assisted by magic, her beauty is revealed, and when a quest discovers her true identity, she ends by marrying a Prince. Most people know Cinderella through pantomimes or the Disney movie, both loosely based on the version created by Charles Perrault in 1697. In fact, there are several hundred different variations of this story, found in many different cultures, with the earliest of all traced back to Greece in the 1st century BC.

A saying occasionally heard is **rags to riches to rags in three generations**. This describes the not uncommon scenario where a first generation entrepreneur from a poor family makes a great deal of money, the next generation enjoys those riches, but the grandchildren, spoilt by the unearned money, squander the fortune and return to penury.

RAGAMUFFIN ☞ RAG

Rags, especially ragged clothes, may lead to the wearer being despised, so a **ragamuffin**, or the earlier **ragabash**, is a disorderly beggar boy. The term has been in use since the latter half of the 16th century for someone <u>dirty and disreputable</u>.

A **tatterdemalion** was another epithet in the 17th century, describing someone dressed in rags and tatters, but is used today in the metaphorical sense of someone who is generally wild and uncouth, or perhaps slightly mad.

'A wandering Minstrel I, a thing of rags and patches,' sings the hero of Gilbert and Sullivan's operetta *The Mikado*. In an English folksong, the wife of a Lord runs away with the **raggle-taggle gypsies-o** to sleep in a cold, open field instead of a goose-feather bed. Sufferers from hay fever will sympathise with her preference, but **raggle-taggle** and **bedraggled** are terms that show the contempt of the well dressed for the scruffy outsider.

Similarly, all the rabble or riff-raff of the community might be called the **rag, tag and bobtail**. This goes back a long time in various forms, and was used by Samuel Pepys in his diary in 1660, 'They all went into the dining room, where it was full of tag, rag, and bobtail, dancing, singing, and drinking.' <u>Bobbing</u> or <u>cutting short</u> was what one did to the tail of a horse, but by the 17th century had begun to mean a <u>contemptible fellow</u> or <u>someone of uncertain pedigree</u>.

RAG-BAG ☞ RAG

The marvellously useful <u>rag-bag</u> owned by every quilter and stitcher has given its name to any miscellaneous or motley collection. We all have our various **rag-bags** around to dip into, whether they contain small ornaments, mixed-up objects, or even ideas and stories.

For a good many years, I have been collecting the stories, words and phrases in the English language that came to us originally from textile sources. You could call it my **rag-bag**. We stitchers fill the house obsessively with our hoarded bits of fabric, and we tell our critics that one day we really will get down to creating something wonderful out of these rags, oddments, remnants and tatters, whether it be a dress, a quilt, a woven tapestry, or an embroidered hanging. This book is the fulfilment of my promise to make something from the contents of my words rag-bag, and I hope you are enjoying reading it at least as much as I have enjoyed piecing it together.

RAVEL ☞ TANGLE and UNRAVEL

Shakespeare used a poetic metaphor in *Macbeth*, when he spoke of 'Sleep that knits up the ravelled sleeve of care,' an image of a frayed garment being lovingly knitted up again to smoothness.

Those who love the stories of Beatrix Potter will also remember a similar phrase, when the poor old hero of *The Tailor of Gloucester* mourns after he has been ill, 'Alack, I am worn to a ravelling.' In the mid 17th century, <u>a ravelling</u> was a thread frayed out from a woven fabric.

RED TAPE ☞ INKLING and TAPED

Who among us hasn't suffered at times from officials who delay and bungle, and seem to delight in blindly following pointless regulations? Governmental organisations in particular often seem to tie everything up in **red tape**, with the sole purpose of driving us to screaming point. But have you ever wondered where the phrase **red tape** came from, and who first used it? You have? Read on.

In the 19th century, Charles Dickens, a noted scourge of courts and petty officialdom, introduced the phrase **red tape** for the irritating delays caused by civil servants who could only stick rigidly to the rules. It was then popularised by the author and philosopher Thomas Carlyle. Wordy official government files and lawyers' briefs were, and sometimes still are, bound together with red tapes or ribbons. Certainly, many bureaucracies still keep *a red tape mentality* alive and well.

REEL ☞ HANK, SKEIN, TWINE, TWIST, WIND and WOUND UP

A con man can **reel** in his victim, and a pretty girl can **reel** a young man in through her charms. Both metaphors probably arise from reeling in a fish by winding in the fishing line. Any thread can be usefully wound up using some form of <u>small rotatory device</u>, such as those used by fishermen on their rods, and for cinematographic film or recording tape from the pre-digital days of cinema and sound.

The division of working tasks and the rhythm of the seasons are found in many old country rhymes; the turning of wheels and bobbins can almost be heard in them, as a humming melody.

> My maid Mary,
> She minds the dairy
> While I go a-hoeing and mowing each morn;
> Merrily runs the reel,
> And the little spinning wheel,
> Whilst I am singing and mowing my corn.

The <u>reel</u> in this case is a <u>rimless spoked wheel</u>, with a bar on each spoke to hold the thread, on which the wool, once spun, could be wound into skeins.

RELIGION ☞ BIND and BOND

The Roman author, Cicero, believed the word <u>religion</u> came from <u>relegere</u>, to <u>read over again</u>, but this is not generally accepted now. Most word experts believe that *religion* came from the Latin <u>religare</u>, to <u>bind</u>, a word from which we also derive <u>ligos</u>, a *ligature*, and words such as *ligament* for a tendon.

The metaphor of a binding contract between man and God has been noted in religious texts from the 5th century onwards. Monks and nuns would follow *religious practices* and the *religious life*, and it was only extended to its more general meaning in the 16th century. We also speak of *obligations* and being *obliged to someone* or *liable* for the help of an *ally* on whom we *rely* – all these words about invisible <u>bonds</u> flow from the same, textile-related source.

RHAPSODY

If you hear someone going into *rhapsodies*, you may feel a little suspicious that they are not entirely sincere, or at least are going absurdly over the top. If the subject of their fulsome praise is your needlework, they are, however, on the right track. The word came from the Ancient Greek, <u>rhaptein</u>, which meant to <u>sew together</u>, and <u>oide</u>, song. A Greek <u>rhapsoidia</u> was a particular type of <u>epic poem, to be sung entire on a special occasion</u>. However, in the 17th century, it came to mean any <u>medley</u> of verse or music and, later, rambling or <u>over-effusive compliments</u>.

In the 17th century, the word began to acquire less pleasant associations with overblown sentiment and figurative *parody*. All the same, much can be forgiven a word that gives us such a beautiful <u>melody</u>, as well as <u>ode</u> and <u>prosody</u>.

RIGMAROLE

As you no doubt know, a *rigmarole* is a succession of incoherent statements or a long-winded harangue of little meaning. How in the world can that have anything to do with textiles? Well, back in the 13th century, there was a *ragman roll*, a roll of parchment used in a gambling game. On it were written names or verses, which were concealed from the players. Strings attached to each name or verse hung down, and the gamblers had to choose one at random, presumably losing their money if they guessed badly. The name of this game may have been a contraction of <u>ragged man</u> from the scroll's untidy appearance. In time, it came to mean any list or catalogue. In Scottish 16th century dialect, a <u>ragman</u> signified a <u>long, rambling discourse</u>, and the phrase emerged, garbled, as *rigmarole* in 18th century England.

An alternative, though similar, definition has also been suggested. At the court of King Edward I of England, in the late 13th century, the <u>Ragman</u> was the official who was given the task of making lists of all the nobles who had sworn their loyalty to the King. These lists were then read out in every town in the country – the purpose being to show the common people that resistance was useless, as so many of their leaders had signed. These 'cryers,' probably fed up with their repetitive task, often gabbled the names so fast as to make them almost incomprehensible, and a <u>ragman's roll</u>, or <u>rigmarole</u>, gained its current meaning.

ROPE ☞ CORD, STRING, THREAD, TOW, TWINE and YARN

Thicker strings and ropes are, naturally, used for heavier tasks, and are made of the strong fibres such as hemp and jute or of synthetic materials such as nylon. It's not clear where the word <u>rope</u> came from but there was probably an ancient Germanic root, <u>rapaz</u>, leading both to <u>rope</u> and to **stirrup**, originally <u>a rope loop for climbing</u>, or for helping a rider keep his seat on a horse, and a means of mounting to the saddle. When you are out riding, the Hunt Master might ask if you'd like a **stirrup cup**, so don't show your ignorance by looking round for a loop of rope, but drink the offered alcoholic liquor to the health of the horse and hound.

Learning the ropes has become used for any set of new tasks, because the <u>ropes</u> of a ship, the rigging that raises and lowers the numerous sails on the old sailing ships, were very complicated. Therefore, **to know the ropes** suggests you're pretty knowledgeable.

You might find yourself **roped in to** something, meaning being persuaded or even tricked into an activity. You might feel it was **rather ropy**, meaning shabby behaviour. This meaning comes from the way certain viscous liquids curdle into string-like substances that resemble frayed rope, and was first used in the 18th century.

On the other hand, somebody who suggests you should be **given enough rope to hang yourself** is harking back to a proverb, and is implying that you are engaged in something foolish, if not downright dishonest, and should be left till the disastrous outcome becomes obvious of its own accord. You might be described as **walking a tightrope**, as this also means taking a risky course of action.

If you **come to the end of your rope** or **the end of your tether**, it suggests you are like a goat that has been tied up. When the goat has eaten all the grass within the radius it can reach, it pulls as hard as it can in the vain hope of reaching something else to eat – a feeling of frustration and of exhausted possibilities.

Sometimes the poetic phrase **a rope of sand** is used to describe a useless endeavour, as such a rope would have no cohesion or strength. In ancient Greece the saying was used as an example of an <u>adynatron</u> or <u>impossibility</u>, in the form of a proverb, 'He is braiding a rope (or cord) out of sand,' sometimes translated as **to bind the loose sand**. There is a traditional tale in which a man escapes from the devil by setting him the impossible task of making a rope out of sand.

When you are **on the ropes** you are all but defeated. It comes from the ropes around a boxing ring against which the loser is pushed, and both the literal and figurative sense date back at least to the early 19th century.

Money for old rope describes something easily obtained, even a hint of it being too easy. There are several suggested derivations for this. In the Middle Ages, the hangman received the rope as a perk after an execution. He cut it into little pieces to sell, since both it, and the touch of the hanged person's hand, were thought to bring luck. It was also said that sailors could claim rigging that had been damaged and sell it in the same way, not for luck but for a more practical use, such as caulking ships.

ROUND ROBIN

The term **a round robin** for a circular letter has nothing to do with the bird, but comes from the French for <u>round ribbon</u>, and was originally a <u>rond ribon</u>. It was a way of making a complaint in the 18th century that did not identify any one man as the trouble-making ringleader because the signatures were arranged in a circle.

Anything long and narrow may be referred to as **a ribbon**, such as a road, metal, a slice of sky, or a type of fish – **ribbon fish** – or grass – **ribbon grass**. In the USA a coloured and folded **ribbon candy** made of sugar is a popular sweet.

ROVING

A rove is, among other things, a sliver of wool or other fibre, drawn out and slightly twisted. The word emerged in the 18th century as a verb in the woollen industry. Still in the 18th century, a **rover** was the attendant at the roving-frame, quite an important job. The word is distantly related to both farming and archery, coming originally from dialect words to do with wandering or straying, used in the 15th century for both animals and arrows going astray.

Other distantly related words came from reave, now obsolete except for something reft or riven in two, and meant to split or tear, eventually giving us to rob. Pirates roved the seas, looting and robbing. There are several British pubs in textile manufacturing areas called **The Rover's Return** – there's a famous one on the set of the British television soap opera *Coronation Street*. They were probably named for the woollen mill workers, but one wonders if there wasn't also a sense of fun in linking the stay-at-home factory rover with his marauding counterpart.

SAMITE ☞ SILK

In the Arthurian legends, the future King Arthur received his sword Excalibur from the Lady of the Lake, whose mysterious arm appeared from the waters of a lake. Everyone seems able to quote Tennyson's description of the arm, **clothed in white samite, mystic, wonderful,** as a picture of something supernaturally beautiful. So, what exactly is, or was, samite? It was a rich, heavy silk, usually in a form called damasked, that is to say all in one colour, but woven in such a way that the threads would catch the light to show up the pattern. The technique and the word were derived from the city of Damascus in the Middle Ages. Damascene referred not only to cloth, but also to ornamenting steel surfaces, such as sword blades, with inlay work, which both gave them greater strength and the shimmering appearance known as watered. Damasked metal work may well have come first but, for centuries, the crafts of the weaver and the smith were closely associated. The finest creations, such as moiré or watered silk, were regarded with awe as almost magical and the workers as magicians.

SCHISM ☞ CUT and SCISSORS

This was a term applied metaphorically to any state of dissension and disunity in the early Church by the Latin translators of the New Testament, who referred to it as a skhisma or schisma.

Words for cutting and the tools needed for it come from three linked sources. The earliest is probably the Ancient Greek skhizein, which meant literally to rip or tear cloth and may be onomatopoeic, the word being derived from the ripping sound. This root gave us a *schism*.

In 1910, the French neurologist Eugene Bleuler, was casting around for a name to describe a type of madness that had a clear illness path. He coined the word *schizophrenie* – usually translated as a split mind, but better thought of as a torn mind – because he used skhizein as a prefix, with phren, the Greek for mind. English adapted it as *schizophrenia*, and we also use *schizoid* for a particular personality type. The term *schist* for a type of rock that splits easily was coined in a similar way in the late 18th century.

SCISSORS ☞ CUT and SCHISM

Here's another vital tool for textile people. The Romans had two words for cut, the first being caedare, from which they derived a cutting instrument known as a cisoria. The Roman scissors were not hinged, but had two blades joined by a semicircle of springy metal, which when compressed brought the two cutting edges together. Such shears are still used to shear sheep. If you are not familiar with such country pursuits, think of eyebrow tweezers or the silver tongs used by refined matrons to pick up sugar lumps at afternoon tea. Because they were made all in one piece, the noun was in the singular.

By the 16th century, the spelling in English was sisoures, in the plural, as scissors had begun to be formed as two separate blades, joined by a loose bolt round which the two sides could pivot. Associated words such as *concise*, *decide*, *decision* and *incision* come from this root, in all of which a notion of metaphorical cutting can be detected. The Old French for scissors was scissoires, and gave us the word *chisel* for a tool used to cut into wood. The Old English word scerero was also related, meaning the action of shearing sheep or mowing grass, from which we derived shears when the word became plural because of the two blades. One can be *shorn* figuratively of happiness, honour or power.

The second verb meaning to cut in Latin was scindere which goes back to skheid, meaning tearing apart, and is also a relation of the Ancient Greek skhizein, which meant ripping cloth (see *schism*). From this verb we get *rescind*, to split or divide, and hence to annul or repeal in modern use.

Scindere also gave rise to <u>skit</u>, a 14th-century Germanic noun, and by the 16th century the underlying notion of something <u>separated off from the body</u> had bestowed on most of the Germanic-based languages their related terms for <u>excrement</u>. It came into English as **shit**, not necessarily something you'd imagine was related to textile tools.

SEAM ☞ HEM and SEW

In a favourite nursery rhyme, a lovesick swain tempts a girl by suggesting the delightful life he has in mind for her.

> *Curly locks, Curly locks, wilt thou be mine?*
> *Thou shalt not wash dishes nor yet feed the swine,*
> *But sit on a cushion and sew a fine seam,*
> *And feed upon strawberries, sugar and cream.*

The fine seam she is making, as a way of sewing two pieces of fabric together, comes originally from a proto-Germanic word, <u>saumaz</u>, a <u>joint made by sewing</u>, and has the same base as <u>sew</u>, giving us <u>seam</u> both as a noun to describe a <u>sewn-up join</u>, and as a verb, <u>to seam</u>.

We use the term **seamlessly** to mean something that slips along very smoothly, like a garment of continuous cloth. By **the seamy side** we mean those things that are unpleasant or tragic – a figure of speech from the underside of a sewn piece, where the lumpy ridge of the seam, like the nasty side of life, is exposed at last.

In keeping with the modern taste for revealing **the seamy side of life** (as in 'reality TV'), embroiderers nowadays sometimes deliberately work on the wrong side or show the reverse of the work, as it can be more interesting and spontaneous than the tidy front surface.

SEW ☞ KAMA SUTRA and STITCH

> *The use of sewing is exceeding old,*
> *As in the sacred text it is enrold,*
> *Our parents first in Paradise began.*

So says a medieval poem, referring to the Biblical story of Adam and Eve sewing aprons of leaves to cover their nakedness. Actually, I bet it was Eve who did the sewing, and Adam just complained about the time he had to take off for a fitting and grumbled about the colour.

Sewing as an activity is indeed 'exceeding old'. The word comes from an Indo-European base, siw or sju. The Romans took on suere, as a verb meaning to sew, which eventually gave us the word **suture**. This is now chiefly used to mean sewing up wounds, as doctors have always displayed their learning by using Latin instead of Anglo-Saxon terms.

We also took over a French word acoustrer from the (later) Vulgar Latin consutura, to sew together. Centuries of Gallic chic have added **couture** and **couturier** to English for high-fashion clothing and its designers.

Some terms are no longer in use, or at least not in polite society. One is **to sew up** a woman, meaning to make her pregnant, and the description **sewn up** or **sewed up** for the same condition was used colloquially in the 19th and 20th centuries. Confusingly, the phrase could also mean that someone was exhausted, cheated or made drunk. By the late 19th century, the same phrase was boxing slang for closing an opponent's eyes with a blow. Describing a task as **all sewn up** just confirms that it is sorted out or completed, and is perfectly polite.

Another word derived directly from the same Indo-European base, siw, was the Greek humen meaning a membrane, and by the 17th century this word produced the English hymen. It is alleged that even today it is not uncommon for the torn hymens of young women to be repaired, in order to pretend that they are still virgin. I wonder what Hymen, the Greek god of marriage, would think of that?

Among myriad famous women who sewed was Pandora, in the famous legend from Classical Greece. You may remember that she was given a box and absolutely forbidden to open it. There's nothing like a solemn prohibition to make one itch to do the opposite, so of course she lifted the lid. Unfortunately, this unloosed all the evils that afflict the world, only Hope remaining, stuck in the bottom.

It was the goddess Athene who taught Pandora to sew, and it is a shame that, instead of being praised for her scientific spirit of curiosity in opening the box, the poor girl was accused not only of disobedience but also of seduction and deceit, for which there is no evidence.

SHAFT ☞ BIND, TIE and WOOL

There is an archaic word haft, which meant both to bind and to handle, but in addition it denoted moving animals to new pastures, showing yet again how closely textiles were linked with other practices in prehistoric cultures. It has presumably left us both *shaft*, from its earliest form, meaning the body of a spear or arrow, and *shafty*, which is an archaic word for wool with long threads. A slang term for putting someone at a disadvantage is *to shaft* them.

SHODDY ☞ FUSTIAN, RAG and SLEAZY

Another part of our not-so-nice textile legacy, *shoddy* was a poor quality woollen fabric reconstituted from torn up rags or short staple waste. It is no longer legal to sell shoddy without labelling it as 'recycled wool', so the original use of the word has gone, leaving only a metaphor which we use to describe a poorly done job or a badly made object of low value. In the 19th century *shoddy* could also denote a person who pretended to be superior without justification.

It's rather a pity more of the old textile processes haven't continued to have a presence in our language. The process of the machines tearing up the old cloth was called garnetting, and an even poorer quality than shoddy was mungo. I'd love to be able to say, 'You've garnetted that job into a real mungo!' Come to think of it, I could, as you wouldn't even know I was insulting you.

SHUTTLE ☞ WEAVE

The word shuttle means something that is shot, like a dart or arrow. It appeared in its present meaning of the wooden device holding the thread for weaving in the 14th century. By that time, looms were large and the shuttle was thrown across with some force, so *to shuttle* became a figure of speech.

As a result, we have *to shuttle*, or *shuttling*, for anything that goes to and fro regularly. That might be *The Shuttle*, meaning the train service under the Channel Tunnel, or any *shuttle service* that takes you between two points on buses or trains. We would be travelling a lot farther if we went on the *Space Shuttle*, while political negotiation involving going to and fro between concerned parties has earned the name *shuttle diplomacy*.

Once upon a time, so the story goes, Empress Xiling Shi, wife of Emperor Huangde of the Xia dynasty in China, was sipping her hot tea under a mulberry tree when a silkworm cocoon fell into the cup. She pulled it out, and to her surprise, it unravelled to yield miles of exquisite yellow thread; it was soon found that this could be woven into the finest of cloth and used for embroidery. Much later, in spite of an edict banning the export of silkworm eggs on pain of death, another princess of the same name was married off to a nobleman in Constantinople in 400 AD. This Xiling Shi was horrified at the thought of being sent off to live with Western barbarians and being deprived of all her creature comforts, so she smuggled some silkworm cocoons out of the country in her knickers.

Perhaps the story isn't historically correct, but what is true is that silk is a very fine and lustrous thread produced by the larvae of certain moths, such as Bombyx mori, to spin their cocoons. China was pre-eminent in sericulture for hundreds of years, exporting it along the Silk Road, and guarding the silkworms very jealously. Certainly eggs or cocoons must have been smuggled out, though not necessarily in the panties of a princess.

The thread from a cocoon can be several miles long. If left to mature, the moths eat through it to emerge, destroying the continuity of the thread and rendering it useless except as silk waste. Consequently, in the silk industry, only a few silkworms are allowed to hatch as moths for breeding purposes. The rest are killed in their cocoons, by being dropped in boiling water, baked or frozen, so that the silk can be unwound unbroken. A great many cocoons must be used to get useful quantities of thread.

But where do we get the word silk? The ancient Greeks called the people from the East the Seres, which translates as the silk people, because they imported silk from traders along the route, naming them from the Chinese word si, the Manchurian sirghe, or the Mongolian sirkek. The Romans called it sericum and the Irish siric, and from them we British derived our word serge, a durable fabric made of coarse wool, not silk at all. Another form of the word, with 'l' rather than 'r' must have travelled north to the Baltic, to sell the Russians shelk and the Lithuanians shilkai. Germanic languages took up the word and the Swedes and the Danes called it silke, while we say simply silk.

··· Silkworm ···

You could hardly find a better example of how a word can illuminate the romance and glamour of ancient trade and the exploration of far-distant countries, than by following silk along the great group of trading paths across the world known collectively as **The Silk Route** because of the importance of that commodity.

We say something is **soft as silk**, to show how just how smooth, fine and **silky** or **silken** it is. However, describing someone as **a silky talker** who pays you **a silky compliment** is not complimentary as it suggests slipperiness or deceit.

King James I of England made one of the World's Biggest Mistakes. Silkworms feed best on mulberry leaves, and he thought it would be a brilliant idea to import hundreds of trees and set up an English silk industry. Unfortunately, he chose the common purple mulberry. Silkworms are very refined, and only eat the leaves of *Morus alba*, the white mulberry, so the King's plans came to nothing. But Britain still has reminders of the monarch's attempts in towns such as Bradford-on-Avon and Malmesbury, with riverside silk mills now converted to desirable flats.

By the way, what happened to the two silkworms who decided to have a race?

Answer: **it ended in a tie**.

SILKWORM

Apparently a **silkworm** was a slang term in the 18th century for a woman who spent lots of time in draper's shops examining the goods but not buying anything. I suppose it's a little like what we call window shopping, but that phrase doesn't really do justice to the favourite pursuit of fabric fanatics, who wander round craft fairs and textile stores in a kind of blissful daze. The euphoria of the emporia! Bring back the Silkworm, I say.

SKEIN ☞ BALL OF THREAD and HANK

Instead of winding your thread onto a bobbin, you can make a **skein** with it, which is any convenient length of yarn wound into a circle and loosely bound to keep it tidy and untangled. The origin of the word skein is unclear, but it applies first to yarn and then to any group of strands, such as **a skein of wild geese** flying in formation, or to patterns of facts or ideas, like **a skein of thought**.

You can wind thread into skeins on the wonderfully named niddy-noddy, which was an asymmetrical frame that appeared to nod up and down as you wound. You can still say **'You're a right niddy-noddy, aren't you?'** if someone does something silly.

SKIN A RABBIT

Here we have a mother singing another traditional nursery rhyme to her baby.

Bye Baby Bunting,
Daddy's gone a-hunting,
To fetch a little rabbit's skin
To wrap the Baby Bunting in.

There are many other versions of this, particularly in Scotland. <u>Bunting</u> may be a nonsense term of endearment suggesting something <u>small and plump</u>, or it may come from the German word <u>bunt</u>, meaning <u>gaily coloured</u>, a term taken into English in the 18th century for a fabric, <u>bunting</u>, that was used for flags and decorations (though not for clothing babies).

'***Skin a rabbit!***' my mother used to say as she pulled my clothes up and over my ears at bedtime. Somehow I always responded to the affection in her tone, and only now, looking at it literally, think that the words are really not very nice at all. Not for the bunny anyway.

Since every textile book should have a *How To* section, here are instructions for making a Baby Bunting robe, sent to me by a hardy Canadian friend. Vegetarians should look away now.

'First catch, kill, skin and eat a number of rabbits, proportional to the size of robe desired. They are best taken in winter when the fur is fluffiest.

'Remove outlying bits from the skins, like legs, heads, etc, so that each skin is more or less rectangular or, better still, oval. Clean the skins, but there is no need to tan them.

'Then cut each one into a long, single strip an inch (2.5 cm) wide, cutting spirally, clockwise or anticlockwise according to taste. Carefully stitch the strips together, end to end, to make a long thin strip. Let the skin dry out for a day or two. It will curl up, skin side inside, fur side outside, so that you have a long fur rope.

'Make a simple frame the size of the proposed robe and on it weave your fur robe, first one way, then the other. Bear in mind that rabbit skin is not strong like leather, but the fur is very warm in relation to weight.'

(The squeamish can open their eyes and continue reading now.)

Isn't that useful? However, I have to say I have fallen at the first hurdle. I am an urban hypocrite, who eats meat and wears leather, but just can't get up my textile enthusiasm to skin the dear little fluffy bunnies myself.

You can spin up the fur of almost any animal. Using dogs, cats, Angora rabbits or goats is fine, because you just comb them and use the combings to spin with instead of skinning them. Did you know that the only way to prevent an angora jumper from shedding fur everywhere is to keep it in the fridge? Preferably not when wearing it, obviously, or your social life might be a bit restricted.

SLEAZY

Sleazy is used to mean corrupt and underhand, often with a hint of sexual wrongdoing. It sounds like a combination of 'slime' and 'ease,' which may be why it is popularly used in the press to describe the activities of certain politicians.

The British used to import a cheap linen cloth from Silesia, once part of Eastern Germany but now largely in Southern Poland. It was a loosely woven twill cloth, limp in texture, which wore out or fell to pieces so quickly as to be almost useless. Merchants and housewives learnt to be wary of it, so the name Silesia cloth became sleasie, and *sleazy* became a word for anything dubious or substandard.

Politicians – cheap, limp, useless for the job, liable to fall to pieces – surely not?

SMALL STUFF ☞ CORD, ROPE, STRING, THREAD, TOW and TWINE

The 1960 *Bluejackets Manual* is full of fascinatingly useless things (to me) about the US Navy, and has got to be one of my favourite 'put you to sleep' books. Lots of it is quite poetic, and even a little suggestive. You must look out for kinks (I should think so) and do things like Flemishing and Faking down with Hawsers and Marlin.

The manual tells me that *small stuff* is a string or line smaller than 1.75 inches (45 mm) in circumference – not really small in embroidery terms – and is known by the number of yarns it contains, called threads in this case. The largest small stuff has 24 threads. Marline is the most common special-purpose small stuff. It is a 12-strand left-hand twist yarn, rather roughly made up and tarred a dark brown. There are other types too: spun yarn, houseline, seizing stuff, ratline and rope yarn.

In the 17th century, *small wares* were tapes and bindings. *The small stuff* is used colloquially to mean anything of minor importance and *Don't Sweat the Small Stuff* is the title of a best selling self-improvement book.

··· *Snip the Thread* ···

SNIP ☞ SCISSORS

A <u>snip</u> means a small piece of anything, but especially <u>cloth</u>, so used since the 16th century. It seems to have been linked originally with old words meaning <u>to seize</u>, from <u>snappen</u> in Middle High German. Both <u>snap</u> and <u>snip</u> are imitative sounds of an animal's jaws, of a trap, or of scissors, and the words are sometimes used together in the onomatopoeic <u>snip-snap</u>. *It's a snip* usually means a bargain, and *snip* is also another slang word for <u>a tailor</u>.

Similarly, <u>a snippet</u> is a <u>small piece of cloth</u>, and the term is used of other things, such as a *snippet* of gossip. *Snippet* can also be a term of endearment for a small child. We say someone is being *snippy* if they are rude or curt with us, and a *snipper-snapper* was a term that preceded *whipper-snapper* for a cheeky young person. Could it have been originally used for uppity tailor's apprentices?

Snick is also used to represent the sound of clipping or cutting, but there are other words around <u>to snick</u>, or <u>snicket</u> from another source: thrusting with a knife. In the North East of England, a *snicket* is an alleyway offering <u>a short cut</u> between two places.

SPAGHETTI ☞ STRING

Unsurprisingly, this is an Italian word – a plural diminutive of <u>spago</u>, meaning <u>string</u>. So you are slurping up <u>little strings of pasta</u> when you go out for a *spaghetti Bolognaise*. Apparently, the Chinese invented this particular way of making rice paste and Marco Polo may have learnt it from them and brought it back to Italy, where they used wheat paste. Or maybe it travelled from eatery to eatery along The Silk Route. Let's hope that your *spaghetti straps* (those little strings over your shoulders holding your low-cut dress up) are made of something more substantial than pasta, or you could have a problem when it rains.

Spaghettification is a technical term in astronomy for the effect a black hole has on surrounding matter. It creates a spiral swirl, as if it would like to swallow up everything in the universe for its dinner – as indeed, it probably would.

SPIDER ☞ LINSEY-WOOLSEY, LITTLE MISS MUFFETT, SPIN and SPINDLE

Did you know that spider silk is probably the strongest material in the world, with a tensile strength, weight for weight, greater than steel? Of course you did. It comes high on anyone's list of fascinating but useless information. Whether its potential can be realised in commercial quantities is another matter, though scientists are also experimenting with spider silk to test its adhesive properties.

You are very likely to know the story of Arachne, a young woman in ancient Greece. She was the best spinner in her area, but unwisely boasted that she could spin better than the goddess Athene. The goddess responded by challenging Arachne to a contest. Unfortunately, the girl won, and the outraged Athene struck her with a spindle, turning her into a spider.

Arachne gave her name to the whole family of **spiders**, the **arachnidae**. The word spider means a female spinner, and it comes from the Old English spinthron, derived from spinnan, to spin, plus the feminine ending, er. So, every time we mention these little eight-legged creepy crawlies we are making thread connections.

Like lots of people, I have a bit of a **spider** phobia. Oh, all right then, I have a big phobia for them. We use **spidery** as a shivery sort of word for something long and thin and twitchy like a spider's legs. Perhaps that's why we try to get rid of them through the action song for children, in which we keep washing the poor creature away.

> The Incey-Wincey spider
> Climbed up the water spout,
> Down came the rain
> And washed the spider out.
> Out came the sunshine
> And dried up all the rain;
> Then the Incey-Wincey spider
> Climbed up the spout again.

Note that wincey was a type of flannelette made with fine yarns and given a soft surface with a nap. The name is derived from linsey-woolsey, with winsey replacing woolsey. So, probably it should really be **linsey-wincey** spider and she could be, very properly, attired in a nightdress of winceyette, a fabric still often used for children's wear.

The spider's determination is celebrated in the well-known story of Robert the Bruce, who was discouraged by failure in battle, and sheltered one day in a cave. On the point of giving up, and full of rage and despair, he kept petulantly sweeping away the web of a tiny spider. He noticed that she patiently rewove it each time and, inspired by this, he returned to the fray and won the throne of Scotland.

Cobwebs have long been used in poultices and to staunch bleeding. In many cultures spiders are positive luck-bringers and represent the wisdom of the ancient mother goddess. In parts of Africa and the Caribbean 'Spider Woman' is the wisdom-bearer of the tribe, and she is also the heroine of a comic book series in the West. Navajo women say that their goddess Spider Woman taught them how to spin, using spindles made from lightning, while Spider Man then made them looms from earth, sunrays, rock crystal and white shells, and showed them how to weave.

Spider silk has been used successfully to spin, weave and knit, and some artefacts of these techniques were displayed in an Academy of Sciences Exhibition in 1710 in Paris. The silk of the spider *Nephila madagascarensis* was produced by reeling it directly from the spider's abdomen (how on earth would you set about that task?), and the filaments from 25,000 spiders were used to make a piece of cloth which was shown at the Paris Exposition of 1900. Unfortunately it proved impossible to manufacture fabric in realistic quantities for industry. What a relief for the spiders!

In the Second World War, silk from the Black Widow spider, *Latodendrus mactans*, was actually used to make the cross wires of sensitive optical instruments, because the fibres were unaffected by changes in temperature and humidity. How about carrying a useful domesticated spider around with you to make running repairs to your clothes? I would suggest the non-poisonous Golden Garden spider, *Miranda aurentia*, as more suitable than a Black Widow, but only if you promise to treat her really well, and personally catch her dinner of flies every day.

SPIN ☞ SPINDLE, SPINNING HOUSE, SPINNING JENNY, SPIN-OFF, SPINSTER and WHIRL

I don't know about you, but by this time *my head is positively spinning* already, and now we have to take in all the words and figures of speech around spinning.

Although home spinning is very much a minority interest nowadays, words and phrases from it remain ever-present in our conversation. The word itself originates before recorded time, and the activity of twisting fibres to make thread goes back at least 20,000 years, to the Old Stone Age, as shown by carved artefacts.

There is an Indo-European root word, <u>spen</u>, meaning <u>to draw out</u> or <u>stretch</u>. This led to the West Germanic word <u>spinla</u>, which in turn spiralled down different routes in European languages to give us <u>spinnan</u> in Old English. Later we have <u>spinnen</u> for the activity, and finally our latter-day <u>spin</u>. Germanic inclusion of a '<u>d</u>' early on also gave us the word <u>spindle</u>.

Spinning and spinners are a staple of myths and fairy stories, all across the world and throughout recorded time. To early peoples, spinning, which turns an amorphous, cloudy substance into a useful thread, must have seemed almost as magical as a woman creating a child out of her own body.

In India, where our word originated, it was believed that a person's level of spiritual awareness was reflected in their spinning. The lower levels had practical purposes – making cloth, spinning to sell, and so on, but the highest level of spinning was pure meditation. It was this combination of the ordinary with the spiritual that made a spinning wheel Ghandi's chosen symbol for the Indian flag, but the same reverent ideas have emerged spontaneously in many places. For example, to the Kogi Indian tribe in Columbia thread symbolises the umbilical cord of the Earth Mother, and it is the men who spin, sitting in a special sanctuary that represents her womb. They believe that their activity keeps the world going, as well as creating thread for cloth.

The combination of the practical and spiritual is not always seen in a positive light. Because spinning is a semi-automatic activity that predisposes the mind to a mild hypnotic state, it has been linked with romantic fantasising. Indeed, the German word for 'she's daydreaming,' or 'she's crazy' is 'Sie spinnen': <u>she is spinning</u>.

Perhaps the best-known early metaphors for spinning refer to the ancient Greek idea of <u>fate</u>, personified as a triple goddess. The Three Fates, the Moirai, determine the lives and deaths of all human beings – even the <u>fate</u> of the gods. The first sister, Clotho, <u>the spinner</u>, spins the thread of each person's life; the second, Lachesis, <u>the apportioner</u>, measures out the length we can be allowed; and the third, Atropos, <u>the inevitable</u>, cuts it off.

For that reason, we speak of someone's *life span*, a span being a measured length of thread, and also of *a life cut short* to suggest that Atropos, the third sister, has cut off the *life thread* too early.

We *spin a coin* to show we are going to leave our choice to chance. It's another way of evoking the Fates, sometimes literally, but more often simply as a figure of speech.

You could be forgiven if you are wondering whether *I am spinning the whole thing out*, a phrase that has been around since the 17th century. *To spin out a task* means to draw it out or take unduly long over it, and derives from the action of the spinning wheel.

Maybe this makes your head *spin* as your thoughts go round, or you may even **go into a flat spin**, meaning to panic. So maybe we could clear our heads by going for a ride on a bicycle or in a car, colloquially called **going for a spin**. You can do this in anything with wheels, but spinning yarn came first, and in all probability, the earliest wheels were <u>spindle whorls</u>.

When Adam delved and Eve span, who was then the gentleman? was a declaration of equality, since our forefather Adam had to dig the earth like any common man, and our foremother Eve had to spin. No one, therefore, should consider themselves superior because they do not have to do manual labour. The saying is a simplified version of a 14th-century verse by Richard Rolle, and was used by John Ball to kick-start the Peasant's Revolt of 1381. Although the rebellion failed, the saying carried on.

The *spinning* metaphor of imparting a twist to a ball or other object was used in the 19th century. Cricketers **put spin** on a ball to make it go faster and in an unexpected direction. Politicians have been known to do something similar, and **to put a spin** on a news story is to give it a slant in a chosen direction to manipulate public opinion. Ordinary people, who are often not always as gullible as politicians might wish, recognise the trick and attribute it to a **spin doctor**. In centuries past, the word *spinning* could allude to rabbiting on too long in conversation, as in the jocular description of a verbose preacher as **his tow's run out but he's still spinning**.

SPINDLE ☞ SPIN

The <u>spindle</u> is a short stick with a weight on it, used for many thousands of years to spin thread, and the word derives from the same origin as *spinning* with the addition of a Germanic <u>d</u>. Shepherds often used sheep bones to make hand spindles, and they were made of gold for rich women in ancient Greece.

For nearly 1,000 years women of the Shetland Islands, off the coast of Scotland, used the same type of drop spindle as when the isles were first settled by the Vikings in around 800 AD. They only abandoned them with the introduction of the spinning wheel in the late 18th century.

Spindles and spinning play important roles in our Western folklore. In one of the fairy tales collected by the brothers Grimm, an industrious spinner is granted her wish: 'Spindle, my spindle, haste, haste thee away, And here to my house bring the wooer, I pray.' The magic spindle flew out of the girl's hand, unravelling behind it a thread, which the Prince followed to find her.

Spindles have been found in tombs of both nobles and common people in many cultures and centuries, suggesting that spinning has long been a respectable and useful activity for all levels of society. The goddesses on Mount Olympus in ancient Greece were reputedly wonderful spinners, who wound mist from the mountaintops on their distaffs and spun on ivory spindles, inlaid with gold. They invoked the wind to turn the spindles and wove the finest gossamer cloth imaginable, which was said to have inspired the flowing garments of the ancient Greek mortals.

Spindles have given their name to the description of anything thin or tapered at each end. Indeed, almost anything slender or frail can be described as **spindly** due to its resemblance to the narrow upright of the spindle, such as **spindly** plant stems, which shoot up quickly but remain weak. **Spindleshanks** is an evocative term for the skinny legs of an old man, and hence stands for the old man himself.

Another word related to thread processes is spile, which comes to us via the Old Germanic language. This 16th century word derived originally from spindle, but later developed an alternative meaning as a slip of wood, to be used as a **bung**. And, a **spill**, which is a slip of wood or paper with which to light a fire, evolved from the same source, in the early 19th century. However, when used to mean letting liquid slosh out of a container, the word spill has no connection at all with textiles.

SPINNING HOUSE ☞ SPIN

Would you like to go to a **spinning house**? That sounds like a happy proposition for us thread fanatics, but it's a trick question, and you'd do better to keep away. If you were a woman in medieval Oxford or Cambridge, and got a reputation for flirting and frivolity, an official of the university could decide that an idle hussy like you might lead the students – mostly sons of wealthy families – astray. Off you would be sent to a 'House of Correction' known as a **spinning house**. Many large towns had such institutions, maintained by taxpayers as part of the poorhouse system. Once you were committed, you might be there for years, spinning to pay your keep and repent your sins.

We women just can't win though. In ancient Greece, the daughters of King Minyas were punished not for being flirtatious, but for just the opposite. Alcithoe and her sisters, according to Ovid, refused to go out and join in the orgies of sex and violence that the god Bacchus demanded at his annual festival. Instead, they behaved decorously, staying indoors with their maidservants and honouring the goddess Pallas Athene by spinning, weaving and telling stories. Bacchus was furious.

He stormed over to the palace with his wild procession of animals and intoxicated Bacchantes, and at his approach the spindles and baskets of wool sprouted tendrils of ivy, and the purple fabric burst into clusters of grapes. The terrified girls were changed into bats and fled to the darkness of a cave, where they still live. Is this an awful warning to those who suppress their natural desires? Or a typical tale of bullying and the impossible choices women are expected to make?

SPINNING JENNY ☞ SPIN, SPINDLE and SPIN-OFF

Can you imagine how much of their time your ancestors must have spent in spinning thread? From prehistory to the Industrial Revolution working people mostly toiled all the daylight hours, and often longer, at essential tasks. One of the most important was creating every type of cloth for the household. Since spinning generally takes up to 10 times as long as weaving the spun yarn, a large part of a woman's day would be spent spinning. Rhythmic rhymes commemorate the endless round of such lives, and must sometimes have sweetened the task.

> Spin, Dame, spin,
> Your bread you must win;
> Twist the thread and break it not,
> Spin, Dame, spin.

The one and only purpose of spinning is to impart a twist so that the fibres can hold together and create a continuous line, and the secret of joining a lot of loose fibres into good, strong thread lies in the twist. In fact, you don't even need a spindle, let alone a wheel. Fibres have been twisted in the fingers or rolled by the hand along the thigh since before recorded time, and still are in many parts of the world.

The **spinning wheel** in all its many forms offers a more sophisticated way of imparting the twist, and is much faster. It was probably developed in the Middle East, only coming to Europe round about the 11th century. The addition of a foot treadle sometime in the 16th century made spinning far quicker and easier.

In the late 18th century the Spinning Jenny was invented, ushering in the Industrial Revolution. It was one of the first machines to take over the spinning process. Sometimes the persistence of out-dated figures of speech is quite startling. Recently, a child whirling in a crowded playground was told by the teacher to **stop going round like a Spinning Jenny!** It is more than 200 years since Crompton's Mule and Arkwright's Spinning Jenny first made their appearance, yet here is the ghost of one of them still whirring away in our language.

And who can explain why **Spinning Jenny** captured the public imagination and not **Slubbing Billy**, the other early textile machine Arkwright invented? Both are long obsolete for general purposes, although they can still be found gathering cobwebs in an old Hebridean woollen mill.

SPIN-OFF ☞ SPIN

There is so much to learn about the ideas that come from spinning that maybe we need a **spin-off**. The term comes from the action of clearing all the wool off the distaff in order to start afresh with new wool, and hence a **spin-off** is something new, but derived from a previous idea or activity.

SPINSTER ☞ SPIN

In the past, an unmarried woman would often have to spin her own dowry. In cultures where almost all textiles had to be spun, woven and sewn at home, the ability to spin well was highly prized in a daughter, and this valuable asset meant she was likely to get a wealthier husband. We assume, therefore, that spinning was highly competitive.

All very dull and worthy from our modern perspective. We still use the word **homespun** to mean anything simple, unsophisticated, homely and unpolished, referring to the sort of rough cloth woven for home use that most women spent their lives spinning. Thus **spinster** – <u>one who spins</u> – and we saw with **kempster** how the <u>ster</u> ending shows the worker named to be a woman.

No wonder we like subversive folktales like *Rumpelstiltskin*, where the mother of a lazy girl, who can't spin at all, boasts that she can spin straw into gold. A King, who just happens to be riding past, takes her at her word, locks the daughter in a room with lots of straw, and tells her he'll marry her if she spins it into gold. He also warns her that he'll chop her head off if she doesn't. She's lucky enough to be visited by an ugly little dwarf, who offers to perform the task for her, but his price is that she must give him her first child if she can't guess his name within a month. Being a fairy tale, naturally she succeeds, against all the odds. On the last possible evening, the King tells her how he overheard a strange little creature singing his name, Rumpelstiltskin, and the King then marries the girl, never realising how he has been tricked. It's really, really good news for all lazy girls, though perhaps not for gullible kings and hard-working dwarves. Since Rumpelstiltskin is a rude nickname in German, meaning something like 'crinkly foreskin,' it may be that the Princess had learned something from the little fellow that a nice young spinster shouldn't really have known.

The British Government decided fairly recently that the word **spinster** should be dropped from the marriage certificate. From December 2005, women have no longer been described as such, nor have men officially been bachelors. It's probably just as well, since the word spinster now has negative connotations of being unwanted, on the shelf, dried up and soured.

However, all women who love thread, whether married or not, should be glad to be known as **spinsters** because of the famous statue of one of the most beautiful women in the world, the *Venus de Milo*. Although her lower arms are missing, the exact positioning of her torso, upper arms, and line of sight make the 'lost' activity she is engaged in obvious to those in the know: she is spinning.

STAPLE ☞ FLEECE and WOOL

The term staple was used interchangeably with fibre as a term for thread requiring spinning, and is often accompanied by many technical details regarding grading for length and quality. The **woolstaple** was the medieval name given to the market where wool was graded, bought and sold to cloth makers. So important was the wool trade to the British economy that the word **staple** is now used for any products, manufactured or exported, that are central to the economy, or any foodstuff that is a major element in our diet.

STITCH ☞ EMBROIDER and SEW

You might **stitch up** someone you didn't like by deception and lying in order to get him or her into trouble. A **stitch** is a little tiny sting or prick, from the Germanic root stikiz, which also gave us stick. By the 13th century it had achieved the modern meaning of piercing with a needle and thread in order to join things together.

When you laugh really, really hard you get a pain in your side, which feels as if someone has put a stitch through you, making you double up. **To have someone in stitches** is therefore to make them laugh tremendously, and when you get a similar pain while running, it is described as **getting a stitch in your side**.

If you are **not wearing a stitch**, you are keeping cool by going without clothes, while **not doing a stitch** is a way of describing someone as lazy. This is not a good approach to life because, as we also say, **a stitch in time saves nine**, meaning that we should do a job as soon as the need becomes obvious. This saying was first listed in a book of proverbs published in 1732.

In past ages, very large numbers of men and women were involved in sewing as a trade, but in the West it gradually shifted from necessity to hobby throughout the 19th and 20th centuries. This change was partly due to the improved technology of the Industrial Revolution, but it also paralleled the rise of the middle classes, in which married women were not supposed to do paid work. It was thought that they should be symbols of their husband's prosperity and prowess as breadwinners but unfortunately for these early equivalents of 'trophy wives', to be idle had long been seen as sinful, so they were trapped in an impossible dilemma. Many intelligent women spent years sewing useless and sometimes ugly items of apparel for themselves, furnishings for their homes, or knick-knacks for charity bazaars.

At the same time, in the sweat shops of the cities, poor men and women were paid starvation wages to work in appalling conditions for up to 15 hours a day, often dying of neglect and disease like Mimi, the seamstress in Puccini's opera *La Bohème*.

Lines from Thomas Hood's 1843 poem *Song of the Shirt* express this misery.

> *Stitch – Stitch – Stitch,*
> *In poverty, hunger, and dirt,*
> *Sewing at once, with a double thread,*
> *A Shroud as well as a Shirt…*
> *Oh! God, That bread should be so dear,*
> *And flesh and blood so cheap!*

How starkly this shows up the 19th century contrast between the middle class woman languidly setting stitches in her embroidery and the young woman in a garret or sweat shop bathing her failing eyes in gin to keep going a little longer, as she sews the ball gowns of the rich. We should reflect on our culpable tolerance of the very similar exploitation of many textile workers, including children, in the developing world.

STRING ☞ CORD, LINE, ROPE, SMALL STUFF, THREAD, TOW, TWINE and YARN

What is the difference between thread and string? On the whole, when your threads become thicker and stronger they are called <u>cord</u> or <u>string</u>; thicker again and they may be referred to as <u>rope</u>. Officially this occurs when twisted strands measure more than 1 inch or 2.5 centimetres in diameter.

The word string is of unknown origin, but means primarily a line, cord or thread, and may have a linked root to strength, and to a Germanic word strang, meaning pulled taut or stiff, which not only gave us **string** but its cousins **strong** and **strangle**. There is also a related Latin verb stringere, which means to bind, which gives us **strict**, **constrict**, **stringent** and **astringent**.

In a wonderful book on women, society and the origins of cloth, *Women's Work: the First 20,000 Years*, Elizabeth Wayland Barber describes how truly revolutionary the discovery of string must have been in the Paleolithic era. It allowed things to be tied and dragged, caught, held and carried. From it came nets and snares, as well as ways of lashing things together to make more complex tools, such as spears and arrows. You could even use it to make bridges, like the grass-rope bridges of the Andean Indians, which traverse fearful chasms. And, of course, soft flexible thread could be woven into cloth. Barber calls string 'a secret weapon' that allowed the human race to conquer the earth through what she terms 'the string revolution'.

To **string together** a series of objects is a frequent figure of speech, coming from the action of threading beads onto a cord. **He can't string two words together** is a way of dismissing someone as an inarticulate fool. Similarly, to **string out** or to be **strung out** when referring to a line of people or objects likens them to a string of beads, even if there is no physical linkage between them. Modern slang also uses **strung out** to describe someone in a parlous mental state often due to overindulgence in drink or drugs.

He's stringing you along is a warning that someone is pulling you metaphorically in a way he wants you to go, without you really having any choice. Even stronger is likening you to a puppet: **he's pulling your strings**, or **he treats you like a puppet on a string**. If you are **pulling strings** you are influencing affairs and people to create the desired effect, as if poised behind the scenes in a theatre. On the other hand, **no strings attached** means there is no hidden agenda or expectations that might trip you up later.

The phrase **he's tied to his mother's apron strings**, or in some cases, **his wife's apron strings** is meant as an insult to a wimp who can't stand alone and is overly dependent on his womenfolk. However, a Welsh saying gives it a nicer twist: **Children when young tug on your apron strings, and when they are older they will tug on your heart strings**.

A person who is **highly-strung** or very **strung-up** is anxious and nervous, as if they have strings like a harp or violin that are tuned very tightly. Similarly, someone who is playing on your sympathy may be said to be **playing on your heart strings**. Being very upset may cause you to be **fretted to fiddle strings**, but if you bore people with your worries, someone may snap at you to **stop harping on one string** or to **stop harping on about it**.

Some sayings are contradictory. It is a good thing to **have two strings to your bow**, a saying that comes from a prudent archer who carries a spare string with him, because it suggests you have a back-up plan and a choice of options. On the other hand, you could be accused of doing too many things, and none of them well enough, if you have **too many strings to your bow**.

A much more threatening phrase is to **string someone up**, because it means to tie a noose round their neck and hang them. A **stringer** is not only someone who makes strings for bows and musical instruments, but is also a journalistic word for a freelance reporter or feature writer.

Occasionally, we pose an unanswerable sort of question, such as 'How long should I leave it before I ask him out?' Or a boyfriend might be demanding insistently, 'How much longer will it take you to dress?' This kind of question deserves the rhetorical response **how long is a piece of string?** meaning that the length of some things is as arbitrary as an unmeasured cord.

STRING THEORY ☞ STRING

In **string theory** we find a striking use of modern thread symbolism. Just as primitive people used thread phrases to express their ideas about life and the universe, so do today's most advanced scientific thinkers. It's as if such metaphors are so integral to our subconscious view of Nature that we cannot do without them. They're woven into it, you might say.

For example, physicists have propounded a theory that all matter consists of **super strings**, which are one-dimensional, wiggly filaments or **lines** that are unimaginably small. Supposedly, they wiggle or vibrate at different frequencies, rather like the strings of a guitar, and make up the electrons and protons from which atoms of everything are constituted. This compelling theory, whose mathematics involves 11 dimensions, has helped to facilitate many recent major advances in physics. So, if you think weaving or embroidering are complicated tasks, remember that you are working, at most, in three dimensions and try to imagine doing it in another eight.

STUFF ☞ CLOTH, FABRIC, MATERIAL, QUILT, SMALL STUFF and WADDING

To knock the stuffing out of you, through a good beating or a deflating experience, suggests you are like a doll or garment stuffed with <u>wadding</u>. So – surely – <u>stuff</u> has always meant cloth? Well, yes and no. The word sprang originally from the Greek <u>stuppe</u>, which denoted <u>tow</u>, or <u>coarse fibres</u>. From this root evolved the Latin <u>stuppa</u> and the verb <u>stuppare</u>, which meant literally to <u>stop up or stuff a hole with a plug of coarse fibres</u>. In Yiddish, <u>shtup</u> means to stuff a woman sexually, and <u>to stuff</u> someone can be used as a slang term with the same meaning in English. *Get stuffed* is an impolite invitation to get lost, and *I stuffed up* is an admission of having made a mess of things.

In Old French, the Latin <u>stuppare</u> became <u>estoffer</u>, and then <u>estoffe</u> to mean <u>provisions</u> – perhaps not so surprising since the French always love their food and victuals do fill the emptiness within us. *I'm stuffed* is slang for having had enough, or too much, to eat. <u>Stuff</u> has finally emerged as one of our handiest all-purpose words for anything and everything.

Now you know that this word has been stuffing up nasty old Roman beer barrels or even more disgusting orifices, would you still wish to use <u>stuff</u> to mean a delicate piece of cloth for embroidery? Drop that word! You don't know where it's been!

SURNAMES

Quite a lot of our Western surnames come from textile processes. If you are a *Shepherd*, *Shephard*, *Shipman* or a *Muttoone* it's likely your ancestor was identified as a sheepherder. If you are a *Sherman* he sheared sheep, while Mr *Witherspoon* was probably someone who lived near a <u>sheep enclosure</u>. *Kemp* and *Lister* were also in the woollen trade, and you all might well drink in one of the pubs linked to it, such as *The Wool Pack*, *The Pack Horse*, *The Staple*, *The Fleece* or *The Ram*.

Mr *Bannister* wove baskets out of willow, Mr *Stringer* was a maker of bowstrings, and *Skinner* was a leather worker, from old norse <u>skinn</u>. *Tanner* and *Barker* were both in the tanning business. Mrs *Dexter* (remember the feminine nature of the ster ending?) and Mr *Dyer* were both dyers of cloth.

If you are a **Walker** you don't necessarily need to get a pair of stout boots and go up the mountains. Your ancestor, like Mr **Tucker**, was one who <u>fulled</u> cloth, and derived his name from the Middle English <u>walkere</u> or Old English <u>tucien</u>, the process of trampling woollen fabric in hot soapy water to <u>felt</u> and finish it.

Mrs **Webster**, Mr **Webb** and Mr **Weaver** were all weavers, though it's just possible the latter lived by a winding stream and did something else entirely. Messrs **Tailor**, **Tayler** and **Tyler** were all tailors, and so was Mr **Snyder**, from a Dutch word.

Perhaps a little richer and classier were your trading ancestors. Mr **Draper** dealt in all types of fabric, but Mr **Burrell** was linked only with <u>bure</u>, a coarse woollen and cotton mix, often used to clothe the poor or to cover furniture in the same way as <u>baize</u>. Incidentally, by way of French, it also gave us the word **bureau** for a desk with drawers and the **bureaucrat** who sat at it.

If you are descended from **Mercers**, you might be pleased to know the term originated with the Latin <u>merciarius</u>, for a merchant, from which we get words like <u>mercantile</u> and <u>merchandise</u>, but **mercer** came to mean a dealer in really good and expensive cloth, such as silk. It is also worth noting that a certain John Mercer of Accrington developed a process in the mid 19th century by which he made threads take and hold dyes better, by heating them with caustic soda. He gave his – appropriate – name to his process, and we still buy <u>mercerised cotton</u> to this day.

Mr **Chapman**, however, was perhaps a bit lower down the class scale. The word comes from <u>cheap</u>, and he might have been a peddler, in particular a purveyor of haberdashery that he would hawk round the country fairs and outlying farms.

> Here, ladies, are cotton,
> Combs, needles and laces;
> For gentlemen, razors,
> And shoestrings and laces.

I can imagine a get-together of all of you who bear these splendidly textile names at a cloth fair, such as those set up for spinners, weavers, fullers, dyers and cloth merchants in the Middle Ages. What a good opportunity for drinking and gossip both then and now.

TABBY ☞ SAMITE, SILK and WEAVE

Why do we use the term **tabby cat** for a striped moggy? Well, it was first used to describe a cat with a brindled coat in the late 18th century, and came from the word for a particular form of <u>watered silk</u>, in which the process of <u>watering</u> or <u>moiré</u> creates an effect of rippling watermarks on a self-coloured cloth. It was made either by a special weaving technique, as with the making of <u>damask</u>, or by pressing the fabric with heated rollers. People noticed the similarity of its pattern to markings on the cat's coat. Hopefully, they didn't press kitty herself with heated rollers to enhance the resemblance.

The earliest form of silk patterning came from Baghdad, and was originally a woven stripe, only later watered. **Tabby** is, in fact, a corruption of the Arabic <u>Attabiya</u>, the name of the weaver's quarter of the town.

By the 19th century, the fabric was not so fashionable and **an old tabby** had come to mean a maiden lady, probably wearing out-dated clothing, who had a 'catty' manner. In other words, she's a spiteful old gossip.

TAILOR ☞ CUT and STITCH

Tailors are really <u>cutters</u>, not <u>stitchers</u> or <u>sewers</u>, and the word <u>tailor</u> was originally a <u>tailleur</u> in Norman French, from <u>taliare</u>, the Latin for <u>to cut</u>.

Something **tailor made** was originally a garment created to fit one person specifically, and is now used metaphorically. We might say someone's job was **tailor-made** for him, or **tailored to his requirements**.

Tailors developed a slang of their own which became almost a separate language, but is now obsolete. Sayings like <u>American shoulders</u>, for a coat <u>cut square</u> to give an appearance of broadness, was commonly heard in Britain by the end of the 19th century. To <u>blow something together</u> meant to <u>make something in a slovenly way</u>, which seems quite logical. But where on earth did to <u>alter the jeff's click</u>, meaning to <u>ignore the cutting out instructions</u>, come from?

Tailors have traditionally been men, and occupy a special place in folklore and fairy tales – particularly those collected in 19th century Germany by the Brothers Grimm. In these stories they are often small and weedy, and sometimes lame, perhaps because men with a disability or poor physique would have had difficulty in becoming soldiers or manual labourers. Tailors also became lame because they sat cross-legged and hunched over their work for very long hours, often starting work in childhood and eating an inadequate diet. Many tailors were itinerant and maintained a useful place in the community by carrying news and gossip around the country. Incidentally, the long strap-like muscle in the thigh that allows us to sit cross-legged is called the <u>sartorius</u>, the Latin word for a <u>tailor</u> (I just thought you might like that bit of useless information).

TAKING SILK ☞ SILK

This well known term comes from the UK and describes the procedure whereby the British Sovereign appoints a lawyer as a Queen's or King's Counsel (depending on the gender of the ruler at the time) in the British and Commonwealth courts. It is described as **taking silk** because of the particular clothing the Queen's Counsel must wear in court, which includes a black silk gown based on medieval academic dress. He, or she, is sometimes referred to as *a silk*. Junior barristers wear drab woollen gowns and are known as **Stuff Gownsmen**. Since they are 'junior' only in name and may be highly experienced and even elderly, it is probably not advisable to hail your lawyer with a hearty 'Hello, Stuff Gownsman'. It might add a percentage to your bill. Employing a silk almost certainly will, as they usually charge considerably higher fees.

Lawyers are not always popular. Maybe we should offer them silk as a protection. You might not think a thin silk shirt would be much use, but closely woven silk has a very tough, slippery surface and can actually offer protection to soldiers. In 1881, an American diarist named George Emery Goodfellow noted an incident in which he saw a gunman fire two bullets into the breast of another man, who fell down dead, yet without a drop of blood coming from the wound. Goodfellow examined the corpse and discovered a silk handkerchief protruding from the bullet hole. The shot had carried it in, penetrating clothes, vital organs and bone, but not the silk itself. He was so fascinated that he did some research and collected instances of the ability of silk to deflect projectiles, including one in which a man's silk bandanna had deflected a bullet away from the carotid artery and actually saved the victim's life.

Long before this, the great Eastern warrior and conqueror, Ghengis Khan, knew of silk's remarkable properties. He gave each of his knights a silk shirt to wear, because, if they were stabbed in battle, the silk was carried into the wound and acted as a partial protection against bleeding. If they survived, they were also less likely to die of infection, which in those days was as frequent a cause of death as battle injuries.

TANGLE ☞ NET and UNRAVEL

A <u>tangle</u> is a kind of inadvertent net, where organic strands intertwine. Forms of netting or braiding may have been mankind's early attempts at imitating these twining patterns. The origin of the word is obscure, but **tangle** is often used figuratively. 'My life's in a real **tangle**,' we might cry to a friend, and she might warn us of a difficult and aggressive person, likely to do us some physical mischief if we cross him by saying, 'I wouldn't **tangle** with him if I were you.'

Other friends might suggest we **disentangle** ourselves from an unfortunate love affair, describing it as an **entanglement** that will give us grief.

We use **tangle** figuratively as both a verb and a noun. We might **entangle** someone, either by drawing them in to a dubious enterprise or an emotionally enchanted state, thus complicating their lives or even ultimately destroying them. **To enmesh a person** means the same thing, but perhaps more intensely, suggesting someone helplessly struggling in a sticky net we have created.

In his poem *Marmion*, Sir Walter Scott famously warned of the risks involved in deception. His lines, often unattributed, have become something of a cliché.

> *Oh what a tangled web we weave,*
> *When first we practise to deceive!*

Witches supposedly cast spells with tangled threads, but you could also use such snarl-ups to protect yourself against their wiles. Here's how: put a mess of tangled-up thread in a bottle and hang it near a door or window, or wherever you think a witch might try to get in. She – or he, as a witch can be either – will be mesmerised into trying to follow the twists and turns of thread and will stand transfixed and unable to move.

Perhaps you could collect up the neighbourhood witches and then do what you do with other garden pests like slugs and snails: tip them over your neighbour's fence.

Only joking. Of course I wouldn't. At least, I wouldn't tip the witches into your garden. Slugs, maybe.

TANTRIC ☞ KAMA SUTRA and WEAVE

Tantra is a Sanskrit word that has been known in English for 200 years: presumably it was imported in the days of the British Raj. Its root comes from loom or weaving, plus expansion, from tan, meaning stretched out. It describes a body of religious writing from Hindu and Buddhist sources, and a technique of meditation, often with erotic content, which celebrates the joy of sexual love as a form of holy energy. *Tantrism* is the doctrine, and *tantric* describes the general body of ideas.

The most famous *tantric* artworks are the temples at Khajuraho in Madhya Pradesh State, India, now part of the general tourist trail. They are covered with painted figures carved between the 9th and 11th centuries, and many of them are erotic. In Britain increasing numbers of healers running *tantric groups* can be found in the alternative health field.

TAPED ☞ INKLING and RED TAPE

The origin of the word tape is a little obscure, but goes back to the Old English taeppa, for a narrow woven ribbon of cloth used to bind or measure things. Other more convenient modern products such as sticky tape and Velcro have superseded many of the myriad uses for tapes in earlier times. We no longer need strings to tie up our garments or to hold most parcels together. Of course we still use a tape-measure, marked out in lengths, and to have a situation *taped* is to have it under control. *I've got him taped* means I've assessed his abilities and qualities fully, and taken his measure.

TAPESTRY ☞ EMBROIDER, NEEDLE, POINTILLISM, SHUTTLE and WEAVING

Occasionally, there is confusion between weaving and embroidery as a result of some of the terms used. So let's untangle them. Embroidery is the process of adding threads to the surface of an already existing base of material. This is often a woven fabric, but can be something else, such as felt. Lots of other things are used as a base, particularly by modern textile artists, and can include leather, paper and compressed leaves. Harder surfaces, such as wood, metal, slate and stone drilled with holes have also been used. In fact, almost any surface you like to name can be embroidered.

We got the whole thing from the Normans, for whom a tapisery and hence tapis meant a textile fabric decorated with ornamental designs or pictorial subjects, which could be painted, embroidered or woven in colours. The noun tapis came from Greek, via Latin, and gave the French a verb, tappisser, meaning to cover with a carpet, and then led back to the noun tapisserie. Norman French was the language of the ruling elite in Britain after the 1066 Conquest, and many French words replaced Anglo-Saxon terms at this time, especially for aristocratic or courtly pursuits. This is why so many of the words we still use for embroidery came from the French language, such as petit point (a canvas work stitch known in English as tent stitch) and gobelin stitch, from the famous tapestry factory in Paris, France, named for its founder, the 16th century M. Gobelin. The art of crochet comes from the French croche, a hook; and picots, which are little loops of thread, come from picoter, French for to prick with a needle.

Later on, in Elizabethan England, the term carpet, which came from the French charpie, meaning lint, was used for tapestry pieces only a few feet wide. These were used as table carpets, being far too precious to be trodden underfoot.

Today, the word tapestry in general conversation tends to be used only for a fabric with the pattern or picture woven in during construction, but it is not incorrect to use the term for any ornamental fabric. Older embroiderers still sometimes use tapestry or tapestry work for embroidery made by covering the whole surface of a canvas base with regular stitches. However, this can lead to confusion, so it is now common practice to call the embroidered technique needlepoint or canvas work, in order to make the distinction plain.

The term **tapestry** is a word often used to describe a variegated scene, such as meadows of flowers, and **life's rich tapestry** is almost a cliché.

TATTY

We say something is **tatty** when it looks almost worn out and untidy, perhaps also with a hint of grubby as well. This colloquial term may be derived directly from tatters – a 16th century term for slashed points in a garment – and hence **tattered**, a synonym for torn or ragged, and also from words linked to matted and tangled hair. Taettec may have been a dialect word in Old English for ragged and shabby, and was still known in the early 1930s.

I would speculate a bit here. **Tatting** is a technique of knotting thread, popular in the 19th century to make an imitation lace, and might well suggest something frayed. Although the Oxford English Dictionary says the word tatting, as a textile craft, is of unknown origin, other authorities link it to tattered. Could it also have something to do with the verb to tattle, meaning to gossip and prattle idly? The dictionary says this word goes back to a root meaning hesitant babbling speech like that of a young child – in other words, <u>frayed rags of speech</u>? A babble of gossipy conversation is certainly one of the pleasures of being in a craft group of women. Another possibility might come from the way the knots in tatting resemble little heads. What about <u>teting</u>, from <u>tête</u>, the French for <u>head</u>? These are all pure speculation.

While the word **tatty** might well come from <u>tattered</u>, there is also a Hindi word, <u>tat</u> or <u>tatt</u>, which was coarse canvas made from jute, known in the UK from at least the early 19th century. Another Indian noun, a **tatty**, was known in the late 18th century as a <u>screen</u> or <u>mat</u> made from a particular form of grass. It filled the frame of a door or window, and was kept wet in order to freshen the room. Presumably such a curtain would quickly get very frayed and begin to fall to pieces, becoming very, well, **tatty**.

TAWDRY ☞ LACE

We use the term **tawdry** to describe something that looks cheap, meretricious, and perhaps a bit flashy. This is a good example of a textile word that has kept its integrity, and back in the mid 16th century folk would have understood just what we meant. At that time, the term was short for <u>tawdry lace</u>, which was showy but of cheap quality. It came from <u>St Audrey</u>, with only the last letter of <u>saint</u> surviving the erosion of common speech to be blended with her name. In fact, poor Audrey's name had already been shortened from Etheldreda. The story goes that when she developed a fatal tumour of the neck, she regarded it as a punishment for her earlier extravagant liking for jewellery. As a girl who loved 'bling' perhaps she wouldn't have minded being associated with **tawdriness**. I'm afraid though, that the story of her suffering was intended as a rebuke. The medieval Church never missed an opportunity to revile women for vanity, and all too often the women absorbed and magnified this criticism. Poor Audrey! Let's rehabilitate her, and celebrate her liking for finery.

TEAR

Here we have a word that we associate with cloth but which did not originally refer to textiles at all, though it rapidly became associated with them and was always linked with hides and leather. It probably came from a very early word that meant <u>flaying</u>, and hence <u>ripping apart hides</u>, or <u>skinning someone alive</u> as a torture. The conjectured base was <u>der</u>, which gave us the word <u>derma</u> for skin, hence **dermatitis** and **epidermis**. The <u>d</u> shifted to a <u>t</u> and, somewhat surprisingly, we ended up with **turd** from this same source.

Many things can be torn as well as cloth and leather, of course, depending on the strength of what or who is doing the tearing. In Old English, tearing had the meaning of being violently or passionately active, as in **being in a tearing rage** or **a tearing hurry**, by a semantic confusion with ripping things up. My little collection of tearing words, such as **a tearaway** for a mildly delinquent young man, who you could **tear a strip off**, and being **torn between two alternatives**, are none of them textile linked. And the **tears we shed** are also from a different source altogether.

TEASE ☞ FLAX, KEMP, LINEN and WOOL

Wool's soft fibres need to be washed at some stage to get rid of bits of dirt and excess grease. Some wool, however, is spun in the grease. The bits are picked out but it's not washed until after it is spun. Either way, clean or greasy, there are two basic methods of preparing raw wool. You can comb it to make the fibres lie parallel, which gives you a firm, smooth thread, or you can card it with a pair of spiky paddles whose multiple sharp points can be manipulated to make the fibres lie randomly in a fuzzy mass, to give you a soft, fluffy thread.

Another term used for separating or pulling out fibres of wool or flax in preparation for spinning was **teasing** the wool. This came from a probable proto-Germanic name taisan – or taesan in Old English – for the teasel plant. The genus *Dipsacus fullonum* was known as 'fuller's teasel' because its heads had strong, hooked prickles. It was used from the 18th century onwards both for combing out wool and for dressing cloth to make the surface hairs of the fibre, known as the nap, lie parallel.

Milton says 'To ply the sampler and to teize the huswife's wool,' probably meaning to apply oneself to the sampler and undertake the act of teasing out the strands of wool in embroidery.

Since the 17th century the term **to tease someone** has meant to irritate or annoy them. It has become more or less a word for light, mischievous pestering rather than real cruelty, though the victim might not always agree. We use it in a similar figurative sense when we speak of **teasing out** a problem, or refer to a puzzling situation as **a real teaser**.

TENTERHOOKS ☞ DYED IN THE WOOL, FLEECE and WOOL

A painful state of suspense is described as ***being on tenterhooks***. For some reason, many people believe it has to do with hanging carcasses in a butcher's shop, which is totally wrong. Others suspect that the term comes from stretching cloth on a frame of hooks, but wouldn't have a clue about how or why this was done.

The Latin word <u>tendare</u>, meaning <u>to stretch</u>, gave us words relating to <u>actions and conditions of being stretched</u>, such as <u>tendon</u>, <u>tense</u>, <u>tension</u> and <u>tensile</u>, and also <u>tent</u>, meaning a <u>stretched shelter</u> of canvas or skins.

<u>Tentering</u> has been part of the process of <u>fulling</u>, or finishing the surface of woollen cloth, since the Middle Ages. Now, of course, it is mechanised, but in earlier times it was all done slowly and tediously by hand. The <u>fuller</u>, who was responsible for achieving the lightly felted surface, got his title from a Latin word, <u>fullo</u>, of unknown origin, which became <u>fullere</u> in Middle English.

Out in the fields in the 16th century, you might have nodded sagely at the sight of huge lengths of woollen fabric stretched on frames and said, 'Ah now. I see you've got the tentering hooks out today.' These useful hooks held the cloth taut while it was repeatedly wetted and beaten, then allowed to dry. The hooks kept the cloth from shrinking while its surface was lightly felted.

The man who worked at such a task was called a <u>Tucker</u>. His job was to rub and beat the cloth, not fold it as suggested by the word <u>tuck</u>. It seems likely, therefore, that the origin of the word here is not linked with ***tuck*** as an act of folding, but is derived from Old English <u>tucien</u>, an obscure word meaning <u>to pull sharply</u>, or even <u>to punish</u>. It may derive from the Old Germanic root <u>stocco</u>, a word that gives us <u>stick</u>, hence <u>to beat</u> or <u>torment</u>, which is exactly what the Tucker did to the cloth. (So now you know as much – or maybe more – than you could possibly wish about ***tenterhooks***.)

TEXTILE ☞ CLOTH and WEAVE

The word <u>textile</u> itself comes directly from the Latin <u>texere</u>, to <u>weave</u>, and the word <u>textorial</u>, from the Latin <u>textor</u>, a <u>weaver</u>, means anything to do with <u>weaving</u> or <u>weavers</u>, though it would be rather self-consciously academic to use it in this way today.

Perhaps we should not be surprised that words like <u>text</u> are directly derived from this and are an image of <u>weaving with words</u>. A written ***text*** in any form, such as the **text** approved by an editor, or the **text** wording of something in a document, is actually a very poetic metaphor that, once again, places thread processes and words in the closest of relationships. **Context** and **pretext** reflect the same intimacy.

The vicar takes as the **text** of his sermon a verse from the Bible that sets the theme for his ideas and gives them Biblical authority. Religious scholars who disagree with each other may throw **texts** around in a display of one-upmanship and an attempt to prove their opinions are correct. However, a **received text** is anything written that is completely accepted and beyond dispute, as if it were Holy Writ. We also say that something is a **textbook case** to suggest it is clear and typical – so accurate or representative of other cases that it could set the standard.

Not surprisingly, **texture** comes from the same source, and can be used both to describe the surface or tangible feel of almost anything, and as a verb: to endow an object with a special, perceptible surface.

Naturists have taken to using the term *a textile* to mean someone who is wearing clothes. This has given rise to a whole industry on the *fringe* of the movement to supply facilities for mixed groups. The non-naturists can stay in a **textile hotel** or **apartment** and eat at a **textile restaurant**.

THIMBLE

Thimble means a thumbstall, from the old English thuma for a thumb. When sewing, most of our female forebears used thimbles to protect their thumb or fingers as they pushed their needles through fabric. Leather thimbles were used first and metal ones were introduced in the 17th century.

A thimble forms a tiny cup, and a **thimbleful** is a very small amount. You might beg me for *a thimbleful of your best brandy*, but you'd be very surprised if I solemnly went to my workbasket and poured the drink into my thimble.

As sewing became a gentrified pastime, rather than a necessity, thimbles grew more ornate and antiques enthusiasts now collect silver and gold examples avidly. I still have the little silver thimble my grandmother owned in her childhood, and it is worn into holes right through the silver, so assiduously did she *ply her needle*.

THREAD ☞ CORD, FOLLOWING A CLUE, LINE, LINEN, SILK, SPIN, STRING, THROW, TIE, TOW, TWIRL, TWIST and YARN

The origins of the word <u>thread</u> are to do with <u>twist</u> and go back to an Indo-European base <u>ter</u>. From this root comes the Latin <u>terere</u>, meaning to <u>rub</u>, because you originally <u>rubbed</u> or <u>rolled</u> the thread to twist it up.

In the Old Stone Age, sometime between 25,000 and 10,000 BC, our ancestors discovered many remarkable new techniques and must have begun to process raw materials in various ways before making thread. Ingenious early peoples learned to use anything vaguely thread-like: animal tails, horsehair, vines and creepers, dried-out animal intestines and sinews, and skins they could cut into strips with stone knives or, much later, with blades of iron or bronze.

Although thread, etymologically, is a group of fibres that have been twisted together, the term can be used for any fine single filament. For example, there are threads in a viscous liquid, such as a *thread of sugar*, or, metaphorically, we could refer to *a thread of light*. You might speak of *the thread* of an argument or a speech, or you might *thread your way* between obstacles, as if threading a needle. *Picking up the thread* suggests going back to something you have been doing and getting on with it where you left off, as if spinning or sewing.

The *thread* (or spiral path) of a metal screw clearly refers to the twisting origin of the word. There is a children's game called *thread the needle*, and it is also a 19th-century movement in dancing, where two participants hold hands and the company *threads* its way between them. Another metaphor comes from the Fates in ancient Greece, the three women who spin, measure and cut the *threads of life*. You might also say *I'm worn to a thread* by sorrow or stress or, in 20th-century American slang, refer to your clothes as *threads*. A *thready pulse* is one that flutters feebly under the skin, like a fine string vibrating.

Shamans and healers across the world, from Siberia to early America, were believed to have the mysterious power of travelling along threads. They could also use them to cast spells and in religious rituals and the making of talismans. So magical a thing is thread that sometimes parents have refused to let their children be measured, in case the thread used for this should stunt their growth.

For thousands of years threads have been used in various ways for healing the sick, especially for emotional or mental illness, and not only in earlier cultures either. Even today, there is a woman in Carno, Wales, UK who offers thread healing for the troubled in mind, with great success.

A story from Classical Greece gives us the saying **hanging by a thread**, for a perilous situation or impending danger – both staples of detective fiction and thrillers. It's the story of Damocles. One day he was sucking up to his king, Dionysius the Elder, Tyrant of Syracuse, and telling him how much he envied his happiness. Dionysius invited him to take his own place, a golden throne, at a banquet. Damocles found he couldn't eat a mouthful; he was too terrified. Right above the throne a great sword hung suspended, held by a single, hair-fine thread that could snap at any time. The young man made his excuses and left as fast as he could and we still speak of anyone living under a threat as facing 'the sword of Damocles'.

There are many other links between thread, love and birth. Moroccan stories tell of men who come under the influence of A'isha Quandisha, a female jinnee who seduces them and gives them healing powers. If the man takes a thread from the garment of a sick person and places it under his own pillow, he will dream that night of A'isha, who will tell him what to do to cure the ailing patient. Well, it sounds a lot more fun than five years in medical school.

We use the term **threadbare** for anything that is poor, beggarly, mean, trite or stale, such as an argument, an idea, or a concept that has lost its freshness and influence. It comes from fabric on which the nap has been rubbed away to reveal the base threads, and has been in use metaphorically since the late 16th century.

But let's end on a brighter note with an Eastern European legend about **golden thread**. In a far away country there is a cavern underground in which dwells an old, old woman, whose only link with the world above is a tiny hole. She sends white doves to fly throughout the world and wherever the birds find someone doing a good deed or thinking a loving thought, they collect it in the form of a strand of golden thread. The doves bring these threads back and feed them down through the hole to the old woman. She spends her time spinning and weaving them into an endless roll of silken cloth. One day, when she has woven enough, the cave will burst open and the golden cloth will come out and cover the whole world. Then there will be no more sin and sorrow and everybody will be happy for evermore.

THROW ☞ SILK and THREAD

In the Middle Ages, *to throw* was the verb used for making silk thread. It may be that when we *throw* a clay pot on a wheel, we are using a term that keeps the old sense of turning, derived from the twisting together of the threads. The term thrown silk was still in use in the 19th century to describe silk plyed into thread by tossing and swinging hanks of raw silk; those employed in the trade were called throwsters. A small shawl to go over your shoulders or a length of cloth for a chair is also called a *throw*, while to be *thrown* or *thrown out* indicates that you are upset, deflected suddenly from your previous state.

The word has been in common use since the 13th century. Probably most of our uses of throw to mean hurled or projected are to do with things other than twisting thread, but it retains textile connections.

TIE ☞ BOND, CORD, KNOT, ROPE, SMALL STUFF, STRING, THREAD, TOW and TWINE

Binding, tying and knotting all have clear links with each other in their practice, although the words may have come from different roots. The word tie comes from the same root as tug and has the meaning of pulling something. Long before people discovered how to weave cloth, they were making knots in threads and using them to tie things up, drag them or bind them.

The tie that binds, *the marriage knot* and *tying the knot* all mean to marry or remain married. We still speak of *the bonds of marriage* and *the marriage tie*. Along with *family ties*, these commitments sometimes make people feel *tied down*, a figurative description of feeling oppressed, restricted and helpless. Such individuals may feel emotionally *tied in knots*, as if they have been tricked and bamboozled. I couldn't possibly comment.

If we say *our hands are tied* to someone, we are making the excuse that we can't help them, because someone or something restrains us. When we say we are *tied up*, we're simply very busy. This phrase is odd, when you think about it. If we were really tied up we would be quite the opposite of busy: totally passive.

We speak of *a tie* in racing or a competition when two participants come in, and *a tied vote* means that each candidate won the same number of votes. If things haven't gone well, you might advise me **to tie a knot and move on**, or to pay a visit to a **tied house** to cheer myself up – that is, a British pub 'tied' to a particular brewery, and hence only able to sell certain beers. Similarly, *a tie-up* or *a tie-in* is a slang way of indicating people or organisations connected to each other, usually through some co-operative effort or common interest.

TISSUE

Originally, the word *tissue* meant a rich, rather delicate fabric. In 1777 this inspired the name *tissue paper* for a <u>thin gauze-like paper</u>, today used as a wrapping for gifts or fragile objects. We also describe a web of falsehood that will not bear the weight of examination as *a tissue of lies*.

TOW ☞ CORD, KNOT, LINE, ROPE, SMALL STUFF, STRING, THREAD, TWIST and YARN

A very early word that meant the activity of <u>making something</u> was <u>towlam</u>. In the Middle Ages <u>towcraft</u> began to be attached solely to the activity of spinning but the word has now vanished from common speech, leaving us only <u>tow</u> as a noun, originally meaning <u>wool</u>.

Later the meaning also shifted to the <u>short fibres</u> from the <u>flax plant</u> and then <u>fibres of hemp</u>. The fibres of hemp are much stronger than wool and are used for string and ropes of all types, and we now use the word for any <u>bundle of fibres</u>, natural or synthetic.

When we talk of **towing a boat** or anything else, we will often be using a **tow rope**. This is confusing because the textile **tow** from which the rope is made is certainly derived from thread, but the activity of pulling the boat comes from a different source, an Indo-European root which gave both Latin and Germanic words for <u>to pull</u> and <u>to lead</u>. The actions of pulling and leading, however, are also inescapably linked with ropes and they have given us a whole lot more textile-linked words, including **conduct**, **duke**, **duct** and **educate**, from the Latin <u>ducere</u>, offshoots of both **tie** and **tug**.

Tool, now a very common word, has its base in the same root: <u>tow</u> or <u>taw</u>. In Scotland, at one time, <u>taw</u> had the specialised sense of making yarn from wool, but then became associated with <u>preparing leather</u>.

TRAMMEL ☞ NET and WEB

Trammel can mean a number of things, such as a fishing or fowling <u>net</u> and the <u>braids of a woman's hair</u>. As a verb, it means to <u>put a restraint on</u> or <u>impede actions</u>. It is a textile word, made up of the prefix <u>tri</u>, meaning <u>three</u>, and <u>mel</u>, derived from <u>macula</u>, the Latin for the <u>mesh of a net</u>.

It is easy to see how a man might have his activity hampered if he were caught in a net. Traditionally we might say he was even more helpless if a beautiful woman had trapped him metaphorically, and he was **trammelled in her hair**.

The word *mail*, as in **chainmail**, also comes from <u>macula</u>. However, <u>immaculate</u> has nothing to do with nets, but came from another, non-textile, term meaning of a <u>spot</u> or <u>stain</u>, hence <u>immaculate</u>, <u>spotless</u>.

TRELLIS

Did you know that you've been gardening with textiles? Well, the **trellis** on which you grow your roses is a thread word, and means <u>something made from three threads</u>. The prefix <u>tre</u> probably derives from an ancient Indo-European root <u>trejes</u> or <u>three</u>, which became <u>treis</u> in Greek, <u>tres</u> in Latin, and via a Germanic descendent, <u>thrijiz</u> from which come all the European words for <u>three</u>. The second part of the word comes from <u>list</u>. This useful word has a number of meanings: to <u>hearken</u>, to <u>tilt</u>, <u>appetite</u>, an <u>area</u> and so on, not connected with textiles, but it also denoted the <u>selvedge</u> or <u>border of cloth</u>, and hence a <u>strip of cloth</u> or a <u>stripe</u>.

TWINE ☞ THREAD, TRELLIS, TWIRL and TWIST

Turning now to another of our set of words, we discover **twine**, a <u>thread</u> or <u>string</u> formed from <u>two or more strands twisted together</u>, hence **to twine**, or **entwine**, describing both the action and end result of twisting by interlacing. 'A fold, a coil, a tangle, or knot,' says the dictionary, in romantic and poetic mode, 'to cause one thing to encircle or embrace another, to twist, wreathe, clasp, or wrap.'

TWIRL ☞ THREAD, TWINE and TWIST

Don't forget **twirling**, a very similar word from the same root. Partner me a little longer and respond to the invitation **give us a twirl**. If you're a man I'm using it ironically, since the usual meaning is <u>to twist round rapidly</u> to show off a **swirling** dress. It was used as a catchphrase by British television host Bruce Forsyth, and said each week to Anthea Redfern, his assistant on the game show *The Generation Game*.

TWIST ☞ THREAD, TWINE, WHIRL and WIND

The word <u>twist</u> is itself something of an oddity. It can be traced back to Middle English, where it meant a <u>branched</u> or <u>hinged</u> object, but it also links to <u>twine</u>, and from about the 14th century was used to describe <u>interlacing</u> threads or the <u>twining</u> of creepers. Ultimately, there are various 'cousin' words related to <u>twist</u> and <u>twine</u> from an old Germanic root, <u>twisnaz</u>, including <u>two</u>, <u>twenty</u>, <u>twin</u>, <u>twain</u>, <u>twelve</u>, <u>twilight</u> and <u>twice</u>.

Back in Victorian times, **twist** was used to suggest 'an eccentric or perverted inclination or attitude, a craze, whim or crotchet'. Even now we say someone is **round the twist** to suggest all these things – or even that they are insane.

To twist someone's tail is to annoy them, as if twisting the tail of a cat or dog. Not advisable. On the other hand, **to twist someone's arm** is used as a figure of speech, suggesting persuading them forcibly. We may even invite such coercion, tongue in cheek, as in **if you twist my arm, I might have another piece of cake**.

A harmless pastime among our ancestors was to recite **tongue-twisters**, which are tricky alliterative sentences or verses to be spoken very quickly.

> When a Twister a-twisting will twist him a twist,
> For the twisting of his twist, he three twines doth entwist;
> But if one of the twines of the twist do untwist,
> The twine that untwisteth, untwisteth the twist.

In the 1960s we all danced **The Twist**, gyrating our flexible hips all night to the sounds of Chubby Checker encouraging us to twist again. Alas, this is no longer possible for some of us, since **a twist of fate** seems to have reduced our dancing abilities – or is that just old age?

We girls might have been hoping that we also could **twist a boy round our finger**, but were just as likely to end up going home alone and **twiddling our thumbs**, or **twiddling our fingers**, a figure of speech for killing time or being idle – and yes, **twiddling** has the same textile roots.

Also old fashioned but still occasionally found in country shops is a **twist**, a conical paper bag in which small objects such as sweets or nails were sold, with the top twisted to keep them in. **A twist of tobacco** is a loose coil of rolled tobacco, which was also once referred to as a <u>pigtail</u>.

··· *A Twister* ···

Many of us struggle to follow the **twists and turns** of a complicated argument. We might also prefer to avoid **a twisted person**, someone eaten up with rage or jealousy. **A twist in the tale**, or in the **tail** (as a pun), suggests an unexpected turn of events or occurrence in a story, especially towards the end, like a pig's curly tail.

A **twister** is perhaps even more undesirable. He (and it is, of course, always a he) is the kind of Victorian villain who gives his luxuriant moustache a **twirl** while saying things like, 'Aha, me proud beauty, you'll never escape me now!' A **twister** is also a small loaf fashioned by twisting a cylinder of dough, and a word for a cyclone or tornado. If you didn't know that, you might be somewhat surprised by hearing that someone's house had been carried off by a **twister**, as you struggled to picture a large house sailing by on a small spiral loaf, or carried off by a villain. On the other hand, imagine being sent to the baker's to get in a cyclone for breakfast.

UNRAVEL ☞ DRIZZLING, FRAZZLED, RAVEL, TANGLE and WEAR

We speak of unravelling threads, to mean undoing or untangling them, far more often than we say ravelling them. However, according to the dictionary, to ravel can mean both to knit up and to fray out or unweave, so it's an example of a word that can mean opposite things – a real trap for foreigners struggling to learn our curious language.

The origin of unravel is obscure: it may derive from a dialect version of early Germanic words meaning to become entangled. We might speak of a looming disaster by saying **everything seems to be unravelling around me**.

Anything in a tangled, ravelled or woven state can be unravelled. In fact, as we get older, it sometimes feels as if everything that hasn't drooped or worn out has **unravelled**.

We speak metaphorically of **unravelling** something that seems intricate and obscure. 'I really can't **unravel** the argument that … (fill in here the words of your least favourite philosopher or art critic).'

There is a story, half legend, relating to King Henry II and his wife Eleanor of Aquitaine. Henry had a secret mistress, Rosamund the Fair. Henry kept her at the heart of a maze in a beautiful garden where he would visit her, and she whiled away her time embroidering. One day, as he mounted his horse, the spur-rowel caught the embroidery and as he rode away the stitching unravelled behind him without him noticing. I'm tempted to ask, what man ever noticed a woman's embroidery? Queen Eleanor, of course, did notice the threads her husband trailed into the palace, and followed them back to the rose bower. She offered her rival the choice of a dagger or a chalice, and the girl took the poison and died. 'Rosamund, Fair Rosa Mundi, fairest rose of all the world is dead,' mourned the poet, and one of the oldest species roses, the fragrant Rosa Gallica versicolor, is known to this day as Rosa Mundi. We seem to remember naughty women much more fondly than chaste ones.

Here is the classic love triangle, and even the unravelling embroidery contains a moral. Something beautiful, stitched with feminine skill, was undone by a spur-rowel, that tool of masculine power designed both to prick and subdue, symbolic of sexual possession. Henry dominated the one he loved, and then killed her, as surely as did Queen Eleanor.

VELVET ☞ PLUSH

The nap on cloth, which is a layer of threads projecting above its surface, comes from a very early word for shearing, and has nothing to do with nap meaning a light sleep. Velvet, originally made from silk, is a cloth on which the nap is the main feature. Its name derives from the Latin villus meaning soft downy hair. The Anglo-Norman pyle, meaning hair, gave us pile, describing the hair-like nap of a fabric, or more commonly today, of a woven carpet.

We apply the adjective *velvety* to anything such as moss which feels wonderfully soft, but other uses of the term are not so innocent. In 1702 Sorrel, the horse carrying King William III, tripped over a mole hill, throwing the monarch to his death. Staunch Jacobites, secretly rejoicing, raised a glass to **the little gentleman in black velvet**, an old country term for a mole.

A much later revolution, in 20th century Czechoslovakia, was called **The Velvet Revolution** because it accomplished its aims of transferring power to the people without a civil war.

Tipping the velvet was a Victorian slang term for cunnilingus, obsolete until a novel and then a television play brought the phrase back into the public arena in the 21st century.

WADDING ☞ QUILT

The word <u>wadding</u> is commonly used in the UK for <u>loose fibrous material</u> used for stuffing quilts and other padded items. The word goes back to the mid 16th century and is of obscure origin, but is definitely linked to anything that can be <u>folded up</u>, made into a <u>bundle</u>, or used <u>to plug things</u>. It was well known both in agriculture and as the <u>wadding</u> used to wrap the lead ball before both were tamped into the barrel of early firearms. ***To shoot your wad*** is a figure of speech derived from this era, which now has two meanings. One means <u>to talk a lot</u>. The other – not for use in polite society – is slang for <u>sexual ejaculation</u>.

In the USA the term ***batting*** is preferred to <u>wadding</u>, but to cricket-mad citizens of the UK that word conjures up trying <u>to hit a ball with a bat</u>, preferably while striving to win back the Ashes from the Australians (and usually failing). The general use of the word <u>wadding</u> for a <u>thick lining material</u> seems to have come into our language during the 18th century. Around the same time, the verb <u>batting</u> arose, used either for <u>laundering</u> or for <u>cleaning raw cotton</u>, presumably because you beat these materials with a stick or bat. Thus the latter word gathered up its cotton associations and travelled to the USA. By the beginning of the 19th century, <u>batting</u> was firmly established there as the usual term for the <u>thick filling inside quilts</u>.

WARP AND WEFT ☞ HACKLE, SHUTTLE, WEAVE and WEB

The <u>warp</u> is the word for a series of threads that are stretched in one direction, usually the length of the intended fabric, to make a base. The <u>weft</u>, or <u>woof</u>, is the thread that is then woven in and out across the <u>warp</u> to form the cloth. The word warp came originally from an Indo-European base <u>wer</u>, from which descended the Latin <u>vertere</u>, to turn, and the Germanic <u>werb</u>. From these we get ***warped***, meaning bent or twisted, and words as diverse as ***convert*** and ***conversion***, ***revert*** and ***version***.

<u>Woof</u> is just an older word for <u>weft</u>, not so often used now. <u>Weft</u> has the same root as <u>weave</u> and <u>web</u>, from the Indo-European base, <u>webh</u>. For many hundreds of years the weft thread was laboriously darned in and out of the warp, sometimes with rods inserted to separate the threads. The <u>heddle</u> is a kind of <u>comb</u> that picks up alternate threads and lifts them up so the shuttle can pass through between the upper and lower set and it seems that it was invented relatively late. The <u>weft</u> is usually a continuous thread, and is now often wound onto a <u>shuttle</u>, a device that holds it secure but allows it to pay out easily during

weaving. The use of the heddle not only made weaving quicker but also allowed the creation of patterns; its development led eventually to mechanisation of the whole process.

The warp and the weft is a phrase used as a metaphor for the basis of life, and the structure of the universe. The concept implies that there is a continuous thread running backwards and forwards, sometimes appearing on the surface, and sometimes hidden from us.

WEAR

We can wear all sorts of things, not just clothes. *Wearing horns* was historically an insult to say someone was a cuckold. *Wearing the willow* was what girls did when they had been jilted. There is an old folksong about such a girl, singing *all aroung my hat I shall wear a green willow*. However, what we are really talking about here is the other sort of wearing, where our clothes get old and thin and shabby – in short, they *wear out*, a term that is very often used figuratively.

Where does our word wear come from? Considering what a fundamental concept this is its quite odd that the word origins themselves are a bit skimpy. There is a probable proto-Germanic word wazjan that can only be guessed from one descendant, the Icelandic past participle varinn meaning clad. It had a base in the Indo-European wes, from which came the Latin vestis, meaning clothing, and it came to us as *vest*, *vestment*, *invest*, *investiture*, *vestibule* and *vestry*.

From at least the 14th century, the word wear has carried the idea of deterioration. We use the term *wear and tear* for the damage caused by ordinary usage, suggesting that everything is decaying, including us. We can say that ideas are *outworn* or that we are *wearing out*. We can nag someone to do something they don't want to until they are *worn down*. And we also describe things as *wearing* in the sense of being *wearying*: hence the poetic *wearifull* and *wearisome*, as *the day wears away*. 'Of making many books there is no end; and much study is a weariness of the flesh,' says the Biblical philosopher in Ecclesiastes, a sentiment that many a reader would echo. On the other hand, an old rhyme admonishes us to be thrifty.

Use it up, wear it out,
Make it do, or go without.

The worse for wear usually means drunk. However, to be **worn threadbare** or **worn thin** means literally that the nap has worn off, and figuratively refers to anything that has lost its freshness or that has become meagre, poor, scanty or even contemptible. **Your arguments are threadbare, your ideas are worn out, and even your clichés have seen better days**.

I'm beginning to feel quite depressed by all this discussion of parsimony and decay, so let's remember the proverb that says **better wear out than rust**, though, admittedly, it's not much comfort. Alright then, let's imagine you have just encountered a friend from way back and she tells you that **you are wearing very well**, which means that you don't look your age. There! That's cheered you up a bit, hasn't it?

WEAVE ☞ BOBBIN, JACQUARD LOOM, KNOT, LOOM, NET, PLAIT, SHUTTLE and WEB

The earliest woven cloth discovered so far seems to be from 6,000 BC – amazing considering how easily cloth artefacts deteriorate. It was found during excavations at Catal Huyek, South-central Turkey, and is a tight even weave, of the type known as <u>tabby</u>. Other small pieces from the site show signs of having been stitched and darned.

It was a proto-Germanic word <u>wabjan</u>, whose base <u>wab</u> gave us the English <u>weaving</u>, for <u>making cloth</u>. But there was another early root, <u>weib</u>, which meant to <u>move quickly</u>, like the action of the shuttle. Since early weaving involved slowly and painstakingly lacing the threads in and out – possibly millennia before the invention of the shuttle – it is probable that earlier words for weaving referred to <u>plaiting</u>, <u>netting</u> or <u>knotting</u>. <u>Weib</u> gave rise to the words <u>vibrate</u>, <u>wasp</u>, <u>whip</u> and <u>wipe</u>, all rather speedy words, while the word <u>weave</u> eventually reconnected with the activity we recognise only in the 11th century. By that time the shuttle was, of course, well established.

It isn't really surprising that <u>web</u> and <u>weave</u> come from the same etymological source. Weaving as an art is not as old as spinning, but its origins stretch far back to prehistory. Without written evidence, we do not know how or when individuals who first experimented with plaiting and knotting also came up with the idea. It's quite a leap to make a grid of threads going one way and then setting another thread to go across the first lot, in the under and over pattern that results in a piece of fabric. There are lots of different forms of loom, and even the simplest are quite capable of weaving intricate and rich patterns.

Like spinning, weaving was such an important part of everyday life that we accepted its figures of speech effortlessly into the language. We take it for granted that we **weave our way** between objects and people, or spend the rush hour **weaving in and out** of traffic, just as the weft threads go over and under the warp.

Many people have used weaving as a figure of speech to enrich their self-expression, including the anonymous Eastern poet who wrote that

> My dancing, my drinking, and singing
> Weave me the mat on which my soul will sleep.

Or, more prosaically, we might say that **we must get weaving**, as we linger over a coffee, meaning we ought to get going and start on a necessary task.

Weaving a plot or **weaving a story** provides a sense of the creation of a whole, in the same way as a piece of fabric is formed out of disparate threads, and such phrases are often used in connection with storytelling or writing.

When you have completed some enterprise, you might also speak of **weaving in the loose ends**, just as the weaver had to do when finishing off the piece by incorporating the ends of thread from the warp. We use the phrase to mean that we are getting something completely sorted out, and resolving unanswered questions, for example in the complicated plot of a detective story or novel. We might also say that the plot of a novel is **closely woven**, meaning that it holds together well, from the description of cloth in which the threads are tightly packed and therefore strong.

To weave a spell is usually a figure of speech, but historically any action involving thread has been regarded as potentially magic. In legend, many goddesses not only spin but also weave and embroider as well; all are powerful and mysterious processes. While it is often a witch or wizard who is said to **weave spells**, a beautiful girl **weaves enchantment** of a slightly different sort over an entranced young man.

Perhaps the weaver best known in Classical Greek mythology is Penelope, as described in Homer's *Odyssey*. She was the faithful wife of Odysseus, the wanderer.

While Odysseus was away fighting in the Trojan War or, later, making his way back, his wife, Penelope, stayed at home. As the years passed, other princes of Ithaca came to stay in the palace, and tried to convince her that Odysseus was dead so that she would marry one of them. Again and again she refused, saying that she could not do so till she finished weaving the funerary cloths for her father-in-law, Laertes, as was the duty of any pious married woman. It would have been quite a task. Such cloths would not have been merely a 'shroud', still less some pretty little piece of embroidery as many illustrations imply, but, rather, a full set of woven pictorial hangings and drapes.

For three years, Penelope wove by day but undid much of the work at night, until finally, when the patience of the princes was running out and her maidservants had betrayed her stratagem, Odysseus returned. He killed all the upstart princes, and hanged the treacherous maidservants.

Some historians suggest that the Trojan War may have been waged not solely for the beautiful Helen, but also to achieve another objective: the capture of the weavers of Anatolia, who were regarded as the best in the world.

WEB ☞ JACQUARD LOOM, KNIT, KNOT, LOOM, PLAIT, SPIDER and WEAVE

Web, as with weave, came from a proto-Germanic word wabjan, whose base, wab, gave us the English weaving for making cloth as well as web for an open work structure of threads.

An early name for a spider was attercop, meaning poison head, which was shortened to cop, giving us **cobweb**.

More than any other of the many figures of speech we use, this one – **the web** – unites the most ancient, prehistoric uses of thread with the most modern form of communication our 21st century has to offer.

One of the basic tenets of ancient Indo-European cultures was the belief that everything in the universe linked to everything else, as part of a **net** created by the gods.

A Hindu story tells us that when the god Indra made the world, he created it as an infinitely large net. Wherever the divine thread was knotted to form an intersection, he tied a small, silver bell. Forever after, it was impossible for anything or anyone in the world to act, or breathe, or even to think without stirring the net and, as they do so, the bells swing and a ripple of music sounds. Similarly, for the Anglo-Saxons, time and space were held together in a **web** as fine and delicate as that of a spider.

The metaphorical idea of the universe as a web or net is really no different from the figures of speech that we have developed in the electronic age. We use the term **world wide web** for a network of electronically stored information, in which individual computers can link at high speed with each other, and both input and download information. Its use has escalated dramatically in recent years and is still expanding.

The world wide web in our own time has given rise to a whole new language that continues such ancient **thread** motifs. People use **networking** as a verb to describe the use of the electronic links between computers, so that we get information from the **internet**, which is located in the mystical region of Cyberspace. **Networking** means extending one's **web of contacts**.

We can post information about ourselves in a special non-existent but accessible space called a **weblog**, which is shortened to **blog**, and gives the user the title of a **blogger** – all terms deriving initially from thread in the web.

WHIP ☞ LEASH

This is not entirely a word of textile origin, as it originated in <u>wippe</u> or <u>wip</u>, meaning <u>a quick movement</u> in Middle English. However, <u>whip</u> quickly became a noun denoting the instrument itself: a cord, rope or flexible twig with which to <u>lash</u> or <u>beat</u> a horse, dog, or person. The <u>cat o' nine tails</u> was a fearsome whip with several metal-tipped strands, used to maintain discipline on board ship.

Scourge came from a lost Celtic word for <u>a long strip of leather</u>, useful for lacing shoes or clothes, horses' reins and whipping people. It gave rise to the Latin word <u>corrigio</u>, and from this we can describe people as **incorrigible**, meaning <u>bad beyond reform</u>, though **corrigible** seems to have passed out of the language. The Vulgar Latin verb <u>excorrigiare</u> became both the French <u>escorgier</u> and English <u>scourge</u>, meaning either a <u>whip</u> or the verb for <u>whipping</u>.

Smart as a whip seems to have been first recorded as a Yankee saying in the 19th century and it came from the sharp sound made by a whip. It suggests quick, bright, lively and perhaps streetwise. It may also be a play on words, as whips made the flesh <u>smart</u>, meaning <u>hurt</u>, at their blows.

Whipping the end of a rope meant binding it with fine string to prevent fraying, and a **whipstitch** can be used on the raw edges of fabric for the same reason. **I'm going to whip some sense into him** sounds very fierce, but rarely involves actual violence, being an over-emphatic way of saying someone is behaving stupidly and needs correction.

For those driving horse-drawn carriages in the 19th and early 20th century before cars became widespread, whoever was holding the whip was in charge – they **had the whip hand**. However, they might be persuaded to give someone else a turn. So when we speak of **giving someone a fair crack of the whip** it means, perhaps rather surprisingly, giving them a fair chance, rather than a nasty beating. **Having the whip hand** over someone means that they are in our power, as if we could whip them. As if we would. Well, only if they asked really, really nicely.

On the other hand, a **whip-round** is not a sadomasochistic orgy but a quick collection of money, often from among a group of kindly workmates, in order to buy someone a gift. It has been used in this way since the second half of the 19th century. From even earlier than that, **whipping in** is a parliamentary term for rounding up members of the British parliament to vote for their party, and the seriousness of the vote is given by a **two-line** or **three-line whip**. Both of these derive from the **whipper-in** of the foxhunting fraternity, who keeps the hounds and followers in order during the chase.

WHIRL ☞ TWINE, TWIST, WHORL and WIND

All the words we use for figures of speech relating to turning, twisting whirling, twirling, swirling and twining are related originally to the twisting of thread.

Since the 17th century, **to whirl around** has also meant to imitate the action of the spinning wheel. If your thoughts are in **a whirl** they are probably confused, as if your head were spinning.

Whirling in dancing is one of its pleasures, and getting a little bit dizzy has something of the same effect as drugs or alcohol. However, such things can easily go too far. In the 1950s, when I was young, I was invited by distant relatives to stay in Vienna for the ballroom season and to partner my cousin Ernst. All the glamour of the 19th century had been revived and my holiday began with a cocktail party so that we could learn the Viennese Waltz. We had to be one of the demonstration couples at a grand ball and the true Viennese Waltz, unlike the tame English version, is danced at high speed, revolving continuously counter-clockwise. I was wearing a strapless black velvet dress and a cocktail hat with black net veiling. At the end of the rehearsal, I spun out of the door into the rose garden and was violently sick. As I passed a gold-framed mirror in the hall, I noticed the extraordinary effect of black net over a large expanse of green skin.

If that hadn't already killed off romance, daily rehearsals were chaperoned by Cousin Ernst's German Shepherd dog, who was very possessive of his master. Any time I stopped *whirling* he would sneak round behind me and bite my bottom. Under this regime, I learnt to cope with the Viennese Waltz so well (there is a trick to it, by the way, which I will reveal for a small bribe) that a fortnight later at the ball I danced as well as the native-born Viennese girls and ended not only upright but also able to curtsy gracefully to the President of Austria.

There's got to be a moral in all that, such as 'Never wear a black veil,' or 'Don't dance with a man who is inseparable from his pet dog.'

A whirling toy, or a flighty and very restless person, especially a child, may be called a *whirligig*. A *whirlpool* is a metaphor sometimes used for a confusing obsession or all-consuming force, such as a *whirlpool of emotions*.

Actions taken while in this confused and irrational state might well turn out disastrously, at which point some so-called friend may shake her head and say *sow the wind and reap the whirlwind*, which is even more irritating than 'I told you so.'

A *whirl* was the term used for the <u>weight</u> on the stick-like <u>spindle</u>, and then became a term used for the <u>spinning motion</u> as the spindle twisted round. These wheel-shaped pieces have been found in early prehistoric sites, and it is very likely that the <u>spindle-whirl</u> gave birth to the idea of the <u>wheel</u>. Think of how a Neolithic woman one day dropped her spindle, and watched the whirl roll away into the darkness of the cave. 'Ah!' she thought, 'All I need is a way of making it bigger and adding a seat and I'll have a baby buggy.'

WHORL ☞ TWINE, TWIST and WHIRL

An alternative to <u>whirl</u> is *whorl*, first used in the 15th century as a dialect variation to name the small <u>flywheel</u> fixed on the spindle of the spinning wheel that regulates its speed. It's still the name we use nowadays, and we usually use <u>whorl</u> rather than <u>whirl</u> for the weight on a hand spindle, as well.

The word <u>wheel</u> has rolled down to us, gathering changes along the way: <u>hweol</u>, <u>weole</u>, <u>quelle</u> and <u>qwerel</u>, for example. Its root meaning was <u>to turn</u>.

In the 19th century, the word *whorl* came to be used poetically to describe the turns and <u>convolutions</u> of certain shells and of anything else, such as plant structures or curving animal horns, arranged in <u>spirals</u> or *whirls*.

The tiny ridges of skin on our fingers are arranged in distinctive and individual patterns of broken spirals. Because each person's are unique, they provide the basis for identification through fingerprinting. Every day, the staff of forensic laboratories diligently follow traces left by such **whorls**, though I doubt if they ever think of it as a procedure related to spinning. Francis Galton was one of the first to create an organised method of collecting and then matching finger prints to help convict criminals, and in 1901, with the approval of a parliamentary committee, Scotland Yard introduced the system that is still in use today. So detectives are involved in thread metaphors, not only because they follow **clues**, but also through their collection of the delicate prints left by convoluted **whorls** on our fingertips.

WILD AND WOOLLY ☞ FLEECE and WOOL

This used to be a description of the far West in the USA (although there it would be spelt **wooly**), meaning that it was barbarous and uncivilised. Was it because of their unkempt hair, or their coats of undressed skins worn with the wool outside? The term is applied in a gently mocking way, and now relates primarily to appearance; you might even say it of yourself coming in out of the wind.

WIND ☞ HANK, SKEIN, TWIST and WHIRL

Folklore makes the link between winding thread and creating new life explicit, as in a folksong in which a man meets a girl 'in the merry month of June' and asks, 'Can I wind up your little ball of yarn?' What he means is made clear in the third verse:

> I laid that maiden down,
> And picking up her gown,
> Started winding up her little ball of yarn.

A year later he meets her with 'a darling little chappie on her arm,' and she demands that he pay her maintenance. The rake finishes with a sober warning in the last verse:

> Now listen young and old,
> To the story that's been told,
> And never get up early in the morn,
> But like the blackbird and the thrush,
> Keep your own hand on your brush,
> And the other on your little ball of yarn!

We are more likely to think it's the girl who gets her own way, by **winding a young man round her finger**. Here is a gem of a poem from Wales, UK. I give it in the original as well as translation, because Welsh is known, for good reason, as

··· *Winding Him Round Your Finger* ···

'the language of heaven', even though most of us poor unangelic beings can't even pronounce it.

> Mi welais ferch o'r Ystrad
> Yn dirwyn gwlân y ddafad
> Yn bellen fawr o gylch ei bys
> Er gwneuthur crys i'w chariad.

> I saw a girl from Ystrad
> Winding wool of the sheep
> In a big ball about her finger
> To make a shirt for her sweet.

Lucky young man!

The winding we are talking about is quite distinct in origin from the wind that blows through the trees, or from winding a horn, meaning blowing it. Our winding came from an Old English root meaning to go in a particular direction, and then to go in a circle, and did not establish itself as wrapping around until the 14th century. A winding sheet became the term for strips of cloth bound tightly round the body before burial. The word winding is related to wander, and the archaic to wend your way. It sounds as if it should also be related to meander, and in a way it is, because that lovely poetic word came from the River Maeander that flows through Turkey into the Aegean Sea. It was so named from a Greek word for taking a winding course, and meander came into English in the 17th century.

WOOL ☞ BAA BAA BLACK SHEEP, DYED IN THE WOOL, FLEECE, FLOCK and WOOL-GATHERING

You might like to know that it was once a term of the highest admiration to say of someone **he's all wool and a yard wide**, meaning utterly good and honest – though I'm not sure I'd appreciate being described like that.

Wool comes, as everyone knows, from sheep. **Baa baa black sheep, have you any wool?** is one of the first questions our mothers sang to us. Another saying links wool to wealth, as it was a major source of revenue in Britain in past times: **Has he any wool on his back?** was a canny query from a financier as to the backing or assets of another money man. I don't move in those circles, but I like the literalness of seeing mega-rich people as fine specimens of sheep.

Early on in the history of civilisation, at least 10,000 years ago, people learnt how to domesticate sheep and goats, and either cut or pull off their wool to use, rather than just skinning the animal.

The words surrounding wool have come down to us from a common Indo-European root, thought to be wlna. The word welnos for a fleece became vellus in Latin, from which we get **vellum** for a fine calf, lamb or kid skin used as a writing surface for important secular and religious documents. The Greek word for wool was oulos, and the proto-Germanic was probably something like wullo, which evolved into wolle in German, wol in Dutch, ull in Swedish and uld in Danish, all clearly cousins of our English wool.

The Bible is chock full of references to wool, and figures of speech using it. 'Though your sins be as scarlet they shall be as white as snow; though they be red like crimson, **they shall be as wool.**' Originally, scarlet was a sumptuous type of cloth which could be any bright colour, but by the 15th century it had settled down to be red, and given its name to the shade we know.

So prized abroad was English wool, that when King Richard the Lionheart was captured by the Saracens during the Crusades, his ransom was demanded, and paid, in wool. But the good times didn't last. The woollen industry in England was almost destroyed in the 17th century by the increasing quantities of cotton coming in from the Middle East. Parliament's response was to pass the Woollen Laws, which decreed that everyone had to be buried in a shroud of good English wool, with hefty fines for those ignoring the decree – presumably, the deceased's relatives. The laws had long been ignored when they were finally repealed in 1814.

The **woolsack** can be found in the House of Lords, part of the Houses of Parliament in London. It is a large square cushion, which was originally stuffed with English wool to represent the then source of the country's wealth through the wool trade. Today, as a symbol of unity, it contains wool from the countries of the Commonwealth. Until 2006 the Woolsack was the seat of the Lord Chancellor, who was the highest law lord in the UK. It now provides a less-than-comfortable (as it has neither back nor arms) seat for the Lord Speaker of the House.

Don't try and pull the wool over my eyes is what we might say when we think someone is trying to fool us. In the days when men wore wigs, someone might tip a man's wig or hat down over his eyes in the same way as he might pull a hood down **to hoodwink** him. That way the victim might not notice he was being robbed.

Don't lose your wool has the same meaning as **keep your hair on**, hair being sometimes referred to as wool, as in woolly-pate. It tends to be said to exasperated adults by teenagers, presumably because their behaviour is often calculated to make you tear your hair out. It is normally used in a semi-humorous way for minor irritations, but many people don't realise it represents a reality as well as being a figure of speech. Tearing out the hair is indeed a sign of being stressed, and there is a distressing condition called trichillotomania in which the sufferer pulls out their own hair, strand by strand. There are also traditions in some ancient cultures of tearing at or cutting the hair as a sign of mourning.

Meanwhile there was another Latin word for wool: lana, from which came the French word laine for the fibre or its cloth. An oily extract from sheep's wool used as a base for ointments in the 19th century was given the name lanolin; of course, the use of sheep's grease went back centuries earlier. There is some confusion in the proverb 'To spoil the ship for a ha'porth of tar.' Although tar is used to caulk ships, the proverb was probably originally **don't spoil the sheep for a ha'porth of tar**, relating to a different use of Stockholm tar, combining it with sheep's grease as a cheap ointment against infections. A ha'porth is the old British halfpenny before the currency was decimalised. It would be worth so little today that I daresay the sheep would regard it as an insult rather than a remedy. Either way, the saying warns you not to mar a job by skimping.

WOOL-GATHERING ☞ WOOL

As sheep wander around, some wool gets caught on briars and fences; it's usually of short filaments known as short staple. Like gleaning for grain after the main gatherers have gone, collecting these scattered tufts was often left to the poor and the aged. A term in use since the mid 16th century describes someone as **wool-gathering** if he or she appears to be aimless, as if wandering here and there gathering wisps of wool.

WOUND UP ☞ WIND

In the 19th century, **being wound up** came to mean being tense and anxious, as if made into a tight ball or like a coiled spring. Those who suffer from stress describe themselves as **wound up**, and some of us have to take up crochet, golf or other soothing pursuits in order to **unwind** after a hard day.

'Peace! – the charm's wound up,' say the three witches in Shakespeare's Macbeth, as they finish a spell. So something being **unwound** is not invariably good. An evil spell may be unloosed in the **unwinding**, as a spring unleashes its power.

In just this way, the sinister Old Foster, in an American folk tale, invites a young woman to his house and unwinds a spool of red silk through the bushes to show her the way. Intrigued by him, the heroine winds the thread up and follows it to his house. Fortunately, she meets her young nephew on the way, and he warns her that she is in danger, so when she gets to the house she conceals herself just outside. Horrified, she watches as Old Foster approaches, holding a struggling girl by the hand. The old man cuts off the girl's hand with a butcher's knife, and with a second blow, murders her. The severed hand flies into the heroine's lap, which allows her to produce it later, in the presence of Old Foster and her family, and bring the murderer to justice. The tale is a 'hillbilly' variant of the well-known Bluebeard or Mr Fox story of a serial sex killer, found in many different versions throughout the world.

WRAP ☞ LAP DANCER, TWINE and TWIST

This word was known in Middle English, and has been recorded from the 15th century for a <u>covering</u>, and also as the verb to <u>wind around</u>, <u>cover</u>, or <u>swathe with cloth</u>. It is of obscure origin, but may be linked with <u>lap</u>, and possibly with the Greek <u>raptein</u> meaning to <u>sew</u> or <u>patch up</u>. In Lithuanian <u>verpti</u>, meaning to <u>spin</u>, is another possible source, and both may have given rise to our <u>wrap</u>, via the Danish dialect word <u>vrappe</u>, for <u>stuff</u>. It has also been used figuratively since at least the 15th century, as in **wrapped in thought**, or **wrapped in woe**.

To wrap it up is to finish something, and it becomes a noun in theatrical slang, as **it's a wrap** means the completion of a day's rehearsing or filming. Sometimes its use suggests a disguise, with the true nature hidden, as in **wrapping your words up in such a way that no one can understand you**.

Other Old English words related to <u>wrap</u>, for example, <u>wripa</u> and <u>writh</u>, brought the verbs **to writhe** and **to wreathe** into modern English. Their word-links with <u>twisting and coiling actions</u> gave us **wrest**, an outdated word for <u>to take forcibly</u>, and **wrist**, the <u>turning joint of the hand</u>, as well as a **wreath** for a <u>garland of flowers and leaves</u>. All these have been used metaphorically from at least the 16th century.

One delightful phrase, now no longer in use, is the description **wrap't up in the tail of his mother's smock**, for a boy-child who is feminised by too much fondling.

YARN ☞ AT A LOOSE END, CORD, LINE, ROPE, STRING, THREAD and TOW

The Greeks used a word, <u>khorde</u>, to mean both a <u>string</u> and a <u>straight line</u>, which became both **cord** and **chord**. The Greek <u>khorde</u>, came from a lost Indo-European root, which became the Old German <u>garn</u>, and by a replacement of the 'g' gave us <u>yarn</u>.

Sailors were usually busy men, but when the ship was running well or becalmed, they could have a lot of time on their hands. To fill the idle hours, they worked at homely tasks: mending sails, swabbing the decks, or repairing ropes by splicing together small bits of tow while telling tall tales – hence **spinning a yarn**, a term we still use to mean <u>telling a story</u>. I've no doubt they also sang, and gave exercise to their **vocal cords** as well.

ZIP

Zip is the sound of a bullet or of fabric tearing. **Zip** and **zippy**, derived from it, are modern slang meaning <u>full of life</u> and <u>energetic</u>. It gave its onomatopoeic name to the **zip fastener** or **zipper**. A <u>zipper</u> consists of two pieces of tape fitted with shaped teeth of metal or plastic, placed edge to edge and brought together by a slider; it can be used as a closure for clothes, bags and many other textile items.

This remarkably useful device has now become indispensable after a slow start in the popularity stakes in the early 20th century. In the 1920s and 1930s, some of the clergy spoke out disapprovingly about its use in women's clothing. They considered that the speed with which zippered dresses could be removed meant that women would be far too ready to indulge in illicit liaisons. Indeed, zippers for women's clothing did not really become universal until the 1950s, although they had become fashionable for men's trousers some 15 years earlier. I wonder what the clergy had to say about that?

A gesture across the mouth as if pulling a zip closed is a gentle signal to keep quiet or to **keep it zipped**. Although this <u>zipper</u> was meant to bring everything decently to a close, it is too **full of zip** to be silenced. This word is going to break out and take its own wilful way whatever we do, so let's go along with it in a joyful celebration of this wonderful world of textiles in which we live. All together now...

Zip Zip Hooray!

···*Bibliography*···

I have drawn on many sources, published and unpublished, for myths and fairy stories so only a small selection of story books is included here. I have also consulted far more books on the history and use of textiles than there is space to list here. For a full bibliography and a list of specific references, please email me at elinor.kapp@gmail.com. Publishers and publication dates are given for the editions that I have used; other editions may well be available.

Anderson, Graham. *Fairy Tale in the Ancient World*. London: Routledge, 2000

Ayto, John. *Bloomsbury Dictionary of Word Definitions*. London: Bloomsbury Publishing, 1990

Bragg, Melvyn. *The Adventure of English*. London: Hodder and Stoughton, 2003

Brewer's Dictionary of Phrase and Fable. Revised edition ed. Ivor H. Evans. London: Cassell, 1981

Briggs, Katharine. *A Dictionary of Fairies*. London: Allen Lane, 1976

Caprara, Julia. *The Magic of Embroidery*. London: Batsford, 1992

Chamber's Dictionary of Quotations. Ed. Alison Jones. Edinburgh: Chambers, 1996

Fairchild's Dictionary of Textiles. 7th ed., revised by Tortora, Phyllis and Merkel, Robert S. New York: Fairchild Publications, 2006

Flavell, Linda and Roger. *The Chronology of Words and Phrases: A Thousand Years in the History of the English Language*. London: Kyle Cathie, 1999

Garrison, Webb. *Why You Say It: the Fascinating Story behind over 600 Everyday Words and Phrases*. Nashville, Tennessee: Rutledge Hill Press, 1992

Groves, Sylvia. *The History of Needlework Tools and Accessories*. Feltham, Middlesex: Country Life Books, 1966

Gwyndaf, Robin. *Chwedlau Gwerin Cymru. Welsh Folktales*. Cardiff: National Museum of Wales, 1992

Harrowven, Jean. *The Origins of Rhymes, Songs and Sayings*. London: Kaye and Ward, 1977

Hochberg, Betty. *Spin, Span, Spun: Fact and Folklore for Spinners and Weavers*. Santa Cruz, California: B and B Hochberg, c. 1979

Holcroft, Harry. *The Silk Route: From Europe to China*. London: Pavilion Books, 1999

Howard, Philip. *A Word in Your Ear*. London: Hamish Hamilton, 1983

Howard, Philip. *The State of the Language: English Observed*. London: Hamish Hamilton, 1984

Humphrys, John. *Lost for Words*. London: Hodder and Stoughton, 2002

Jack, Albert. *Red Herrings and White Elephants*. London: Metro Publishing, 2004

Jenkins, Mary and Claridge, Clare. *Making Welsh Quilts: The Textile Tradition that Inspired the Amish?* Newton Abbot: David and Charles, 2005

McGrath, Sheena. *The Sun Goddess*. London: Blandford, 1977

Opie, Iona and Peter. *The Oxford Dictionary of Nursery Rhymes*. Oxford: Oxford University Press, 1975

Oxford Companion to Fairy Tales. Ed. Zipes, Jack. Oxford: Oxford University Press, 2000

Oxford English Dictionary. 2nd ed. Oxford: Clarendon Press, 1989

Paine, Sheila. *Embroidered Textiles: Traditional Patterns from Five Continents*. London: Thames and Hudson, 1990.

Partridge, Eric. *A Dictionary of Historical Slang*. Abridged ed. London: Penguin Books, 1972

Procter, Molly G. *Needlework Tools and Accessories*. London: Batsford, 1990

Rees, Nigel. *Cassell Dictionary of Catchphrases*. London: Cassell, 1996

Rees, Nigel. *Cassell Dictionary of Word and Phrase Origins*. London: Cassell, 1996

Roberts, Chris. *Heavy Words Lightly Thrown: The Reason behind the Rhyme?* London: F & M Publications, 2003

Rogers, James. *The Dictionary of Clichés*. New York: Ballantine Books, 1988

Schoesor, Mary. *World Textiles: A Concise History*. London: Thames and Hudson, 2003

Schwartz, Alvin. *Cross Your Fingers and Spit in Your Hat: Superstitions and Other Beliefs*. London: Andre Deutsch, 1976

Shorter Oxford English Dictionary. Oxford: Clarendon Press, 1973

Stevens, Helen M. *The Myth and Magic of Embroidery*. Newton Abbot: David and Charles, 1999

Trubshaw, Bob. *Explore Folklore*. Loughborough: Heart of Albion Press, 2003

Wayland Barber, Elizabeth. *Women's Work: The First 20,000 Years*. New York: W.W. Norton and Co., 1994

Williamson, Robin. *The Craneskin Bag: Celtic Stories and Poems*. Edinburgh: Canongate, 1989.

···*Index*···

This is an index of the words and phrases discussed in the book, plus the various names mentioned and topics covered. **Bold** page numbers indicate main entries. To avoid long lists beginning with the same word and giving the same page number, some phrases have been indexed using only their key words. Most of the phrases using a particular key word will be found in its main entry. Where variations on the key word are listed (eg. wear/wearing) then they are placed in the index by the spelling of the first word only. Source words in languages other than English have not normally been indexed.

hackney cab 49
haft 96
hair, trammelled in her 130
hair on, keep your 146
hair out, tear your 146-7
hair sieve 39
Hakon of Denmark 34
Hamlet 16, 49
hand, whip 141
handle 49
hang/hanging 49, 50, 60, 90,
    114, 127
hangman's perks 91
hank **49**
hanker 49
ha'porth of tar, spoil the ship
    for a 147
hard lines 62
harping on 114
hat, all around my 136
hat pins 78
hay needle 71
haystack, needle in a 71
head is spinning 105
head line 60
head of a pin, angels dancing
    on the 78
headline 61
healing, thread 126
hear a pin drop 78
heart line 60
heart strings 113, 114
heck, by 49
heckle/heckling 48
heddle 48, 51, 135, 136
heirloom 67
hem/hemmed in **49**
hemp/hempen **50**, 65, 129
Henry I, King 35
Henry II, King 133-4
Henry VIII, King 58
Hercules 18
high cotton 28
highly-strung 114
Hindu myths & legends 139
holding the line 62
Homer 13, 138
homespuns, hempen 50
Hood, Thomas 112
hoodwink 146
horns, wearing 136
hot line 63
hotel, textile 125
House of Lords 31, 146
house, spinning **108**
house, tied 129
Huangde, Emperor 97
Hunt, Leigh 78
hurry, tearing 123
hymen 95

immaculate 130
impliable 80

implicate 81
imply 80
Impressionists 81
Incey-Wincey spider 104
incision 93
incorrigible 140
Indra 139
inkling/inkles/inkle-weavers
    50-1
internet 140
Inuit string games 21
invest/investiture 136
Iphitus 18
Isaac & Rebekah 41
Island of Women 44

Jack be nimble 58
Jacob 41
Jacob's sheep 42
Jacquard, Joseph-Marie 51
jacquard loom **51**
James I, King 99
Jason & the Argonauts 42-3
jeff's click, alter the 117
Jenny, Spinning **109-10**
jokes 55, 99
journalism, cheque-book 35
judge, line 60
jumpers see sweaters

Kama Sutra **52**
kangaroo 55
Katherine of Aragon 58
kemp/kempt/kempster **52-3**,
    54, 55, 110, 115
King's Counsel 118
Kington, Miles 12
Klotho (Fates) 22, 60, 106,
    126
knit/knitting **53-5**
knitters of Dent, terrible 53
knitting madonnas 53
knob 55
knock the stuffing out of 115
knoll 55
knot/knotting/knotted 53, 54,
    55-7, 128, 129
knotgrass 55
knothole 55
knots per hour 56
knotty problem 57
knout 56
know the ropes 90
knuckle 55

lace/lacing/lacy **57-8**, 122
lace-piece 58
Lachesis (Fates) 22, 60, 106,
    126
Lady of the Lake 92
lam 13-14

lamb, Mary had a little 42
lambast 13
lamb's-wool 42
lane, filter 39
Langland, William 70
lanolin 147
lap **59**
lap dancer **59**
lap dog 59
lash/lashing 59, 140
lasso 57, 58
latch 58
laugh himself into/have some-
    one in stitches 34, 111
laws 37, 146
lawyers 118
laying it on the line 63
learning the ropes 90
lease 59
leash **59**
leaves of a book 52
legends see fairy tales & folk
    tales; myths & legends
Lewis, C.S. 51
Lewis, Esther 71
liable 89
lies, patchwork of 74
lies, tissue of 129
life cut short 106
life expectancy 69
life, seamy side of 94
life span 106
life thread/threads of life 25,
    106, 126
life, web of 37
lifeline 60
life's rich tapestry 121
lifestyle, plush 79
ligament 89
ligature 89
light, thread of 126
lightning, bead 14
line/lines 44, **60-4**
line-up 60
lineage 62
lineaments 62
lineman 64
linen 60, **64-5**
lingerie 64
linguistic shifts 41, 55, 65, 122
lining 60, 61, 63, 64
linnet 64
linoleum 64
linseed oil 64
linsey-woolsey/linsey-wincey
    67, 104
lint 64
lip, button your 19
lister 115
little gentleman in black velvet
    134
Little Miss Muffett **69**
Little Red Riding Hood 77-8
Loki 73

patch/patching/patchy 23, **74-5**
patchery 74
patchwork 74-5, 82
peace, bound over to keep the 15
Peasants Revolt 107
peat 74
peddlers 116
Penelope 138-9
Penn, William 83
Pepys, Samuel 78, 87
Perkin, Sir William 18
perplexed 80
Perrault, Charles 86
Persian myths & legends 65
person, twisted 133
petit point 121
pickin', cotton-pickin' minute 28
picking up the thread 126
picots 121
piece of string, how long is 114
piece/piecing 74, **75**
piecener 75
pigtail 131
pile 134
pin/pins 69, 71, **75-8**
pin money 76-7
pin-up 78
pinafore 76
pinhead 76
pinpoint 76
pinprick 76
pins & needles 71, 76
pirates 92
piss, taking the 73
plait/plaiting **78-9**, 80, 137
playing on your heart strings 114
pleat 79
pliable/pliant 80
pliers 80
plight/plighting **79**
Pliny the Elder 28
plot, weaving a 138
plumbline 60
plush **79**
ply/plying 63, 78, **79-81**, 125
plywood 81
pockets, lining your 61
poetry & verse quotations 33, 34, 63, 64, 69, 71, 77, 78, 92, 94, 107, 112, 119, 123, 138, 145
point 76
pointillism **81**
Polo, Marco 103
Pontcysyllte aqueduct 40
Pop goes the weasel **81-2**
popular songs & rhymes 64, 68, 69, 81, 87, 88, 109, 116, 136, 143
see also nursery rhymes

posies & nosegays 19, 56
pot on a wheel, throw a 128
Potter, Beatrix 88
prayers 13, 14
precedent, bound by 15
pretext 125
problem, knotty 57
profit, netting a 73
promise, binding 15
prosody 89
proverbs 12, 14, 15, 20, 23, 77, 90, 91, 111, 113, 137, 147
public, don't wash your dirty linen in 65
pubs & pub names 92, 115, 129
Puccini, Giacomo 112
pull the wool over my eyes 146
pulling strings/your strings 113
pulp fiction 85
pulse, thready 126
punch, lamb's-wool 42
punched cards 51
puppet on a string 113
purple **18**
put spin on/put a spin on 107
putting out a fleece 42

Quakers 30, 83
Queen's Counsel 118
quilt/quilting **82-3**
quilting bee 29, 82
quotations
    Bible 12, 62, 71, 136, 146
    Chaucer 33
    Congreve 27
    Fowler 64
    Gilbert & Sullivan 87
    Gudrunarkvida 34
    Hood 112
    Hunt 78
    Lewis 71
    Milton 34, 63, 123
    Pepys 87
    Pliny 28
    Potter 88
    Scott 119
    Shakespeare 16, 30, 87, 147
    Tennyson 92
    Yeats 33
    see also poetry & verse quotations

rabbits 28, 45, **100-1**
race, tied 129
rag/ragged/rags 23, **84-6**
rag-bag **87**
rag, tag & bobtail 87
ragabash 86
ragamuffin **86-7**

rage, in a tearing 123
Ragged Robin 84
Raggedy-Ann 84
raggle taggle gypsies-o 87
ragman roll 89-90
ragtime 84
railway lines 60
rain, bound to 15
rash, nettle 47
rather ropy 90
ravel/ravelling **87-8**, 133
read between the lines 61
real teaser 123
Rebekah & Isaac 41
received text 125
red hackle 48
red rag 85
Red Riding Hood 77-8
red tape **88**
Redfern, Anthea 130
reel **88**
regimental hackles 48
religion/religious **89**
rely 89
remnant 73
rescind 93
rest, cut above the 29
restaurant, textile 125
retting flax 65
revert 135
revolutions 107, 134
rhapsody **89**
rhymes *see* nursery rhymes; popular songs & rhymes; tongue-twisters
rhyming slang 70, 82
ribbon 91
rich tapestry, life's 121
Richard the Lionheart, King 146
riches, rags to 86
riding the rag 86
right niddy-noddy 99
rigmarole **89-90**
riven 92
road, corduroy 27
'road map' quilts 83
robbers, band of 13
robe, Baby Bunting 100
Robert the Bruce 104
robin, round **91**
Rockingham, Marquis of 71
rod & line 60
rolag 54
Rolle, Richard 107
rope/roped/ropy 50, 65, **90-1**, 112, 113, 129, 140
    sheets 11, 24
Rosamund the Fair 133-4
rosaries 14
round robin **91**
round the twist 131
rove/rover/roving 75, **92**
royal purple 18